YOU MIGHT DIE TOMORROW

SO LIVE TODAY

FACE YOUR FEAR OF DEATH TO
LIVE YOUR MOST MEANINGFUL LIFE

KATE MANSER

HIGHLINE
HOUSE

For Mom and Dad.
Thank you for allowing me to try the trombone in fifth grade.
It was ridiculous, but you let me figure that out for myself.

Before we get started:

Take a deep breath and look up at the sky.
Close your eyes. Put your hand over your heart.
Allow a smile to spread across your face, and say:

"Hey, I'm alive."

CONTENTS

PART I:

LEARN FROM MY RADICAL AWAKING

PART II:

LEARN FROM PEOPLE WHO HAVE BEEN THERE

PART III:

HACK YOUR FEAR OF DEATH

PART IV:

HOW TO FACE DEATH AND
FIND YOUR MEANINGFUL THINGS

CONCLUSION

PROLOGUE

I am convinced I'm on the edge of death as the result of a brain-eating amoeba with a 99% fatality rate. There are only about three cases of people surviving this thing. Ever. The amoeba lives in warm freshwater and travels up to your brain through your nose, where it starts munching away at your brain cells until you die.

My sister and I are in New Zealand. It's June — winter there — just after the summer rush and before the skiers converge. The pièce de résistance of our Sister Soul Adventure was a two-day mountain trek in the Southern Alps — the first multi-day hike either of us had ever done.

The journey to our camping spot for the night was eight hours of we-definitely-didn't-think-it-would-be-this-hard hiking with all our necessities carried on our backs: food, blankets, and of course, a bottle of wine. Each. But Kelly and I survived, and eventually arrived at our destination: a lone metal hut deep in the Copland Valley. No heat, no food, no beds, and no other people besides the live-in volunteer ranger. Just us and a blanket on the floor.

We built our entire trip around this particular trek for one reason. Just a short walk from the hut was a geothermal pool, a hot tub in the ground, created by water runoff from the mountain heated by the earth's crust. Warm, healing water to nurse our exhausted muscles.

As quickly as we could in the frigid air and darkening hut, we peeled off our muddy trekking clothes and slipped on our bathing suits. The damp mountain air clung to our skin as we skittered the hundred yards down the hill to the pools. Everything that was verdant green around us was now turning black with night. Cold water droplets formed and perched on everything that stood still. The last breath of light retreated behind the rugged mountains. As we walked, flickering stars were the only aid to our dim flashlights.

The pools looked ghostly and from another planet, like craters in the ground filled with smoky, bubbling liquid. Our eyes traced the chain of three perfectly round watery pools to their tributary, a dark, serpentine flow which disappeared into wooded darkness at the base of the mountain peaks. Like the back of a Spinosaurus, the high mountains formed a sharp ridge around the pools. In the center, the glistening mist seemed to hang in the starlight.

As we examined our surroundings, our flashlights landed on a sign at the side of the pool:

WARNING:
Do Not Allow Water to Enter Your Nose
NAEGLERIA FOWLERI
An Amoeba Common to Thermal Pools May Enter
Causing a Rare Infection and Death

Kelly and I exchanged worried glances, then shined our flashlights through the mist and across the pools one last time. We nodded to each other, and with equal parts exhilaration and trepidation, eased in, step by steaming step.

The warm, gently bubbling natural water did exactly what we had hoped, melting away the tension in our muscles created by the long day of uphill hiking.

It was, however, a very shallow crater. We soaked flat on our bellies in less than a foot of water, rooting down in the silt to immerse our bodies, only our heads above water. It had become pitch black outside and was near freezing. All I could see was the thick, wafting, spirit-like sheets of steam rising in the night sky. We closed our eyes and breathed it all in. *This* is what we had come for.

Apparently, the only way you can contract the amoeba is if the infected water is insufflated (good word) deep into your nasal passages where the amoeba can attach itself to the olfactory nerves up in your brain. They start having dinner up there, and with doctors having less than a 1% chance of saving you, no more than eighteen days later, you're dead.

The Department of Conservation warning sign outside the pool had said not to dunk your head underwater to avoid contracting the *primary amoebic meningoencephalitis*. And I didn't — my nose never touched the water.

But the next day, I started feeling sick and I did what any modern person does when confronting a health scare: I turned to Google for some light reading of 439 articles about the suspected condition. I had many of the amoebic meningitis symptoms: a sore throat, a headache, a stiff neck…a tingling in the top of my spine, possibly. And was that headache concentrated in my frontal lobe? I worried that I had contracted it in the pool when I *may have* scratched my nose with my finger, and that's how I was going to die. From a nose scratch. Or maybe the amoeba could live in the mist that had been continuously steaming up from the water right into my nasal passages.

I looked up from my Google search results. *I could die in less than eighteen days*, I thought. My next thought hit me:

"*I can't die. I haven't finished my book.*"

In the face of death, this is the single thought that came to me. Death had shined a light on what was truly important to me.

But this amoeba was going to kill me in just a few days. I'd been procrastinating writing for months. I didn't have a quarter of the book finished. Now that the amoeba had gotten me, I had missed my chance. I had procrastinated for too long.

But you know what? For that week that I was convinced I had only a few days left to live, every day I woke up, I was *thrilled*. I made it another day! I awoke overcome with gratitude to be *not dead*. I savored the flavor of my morning coffee. I worried less about money and yet had no interest in buying new stuff. I accepted another piece of chocolate. Traveling with my sister, I realized I would be content to die doing something special and meaningful with her. Life suddenly felt precious and sweet.

Still alive after a week, I realized that I was most likely just getting a cold. But I wouldn't trade my phantom brain-eating amoeba experience for anything. In the face of a fatal disease, imaginary or not, I experienced raw gratitude for being alive and crystal clarity about what's meaningful to me.

My hypochondriacal amoeba incident was not my radical awakening to the power of death in life; that came a year earlier. But I look at the amoeba experience as more of a necessary refresher, because living like you might die tomorrow is a daily mindset which requires active, ongoing maintenance. I share this story with you because how I felt when I thought I was dying — present, vibrant, grateful, and urgent to live — epitomizes how you can feel after taking in the lessons contained in this book.

Since I didn't die, you hold this book in your hands now. I have written it to help you understand what it means to you to live every day like you might die tomorrow.

◻

EXPOSURE THERAPY

Every single one of us is walking around with a terminal disease.

It's called life.

Your neighbor with leukemia might be given six months to live, but you could die next week in perfect health.

Death may come unexpectedly, and it often does — in everyday or peculiar ways. A high school kid golfing the sixth hole at a course in New York swung his club into a bench in frustration. The shaft snapped, bounced back, and pierced him in the heart. A farmer in Brazil was lying in bed when a cow, who had been grazing on the hill behind the home, stepped onto the roof and fell through, landing directly on the sleeping farmer. His wife, who had been sleeping next to him, and the cow were unharmed. A seven-year-old girl was killed when struck in the head by a stone during a visit to the zoo. The stone was thrown by an elephant. *By an elephant.*

My 27-year-old friend Mallory was walking across the street when a drunk driver mowed her down and killed her. Another friend of mine, Noah, was only 29 when he didn't wake up the morning after Christmas. He had died in his sleep.

You are going to die. Everyone you know is going to die. Do you have kids? They are going to die, too. So will their kids' kids.

Earth as we know it may cease to exist. A volcano could blow and decimate an entire country. California could end up underwater. A plague-esque epidemic could kill an entire population. The sun could go out like a light bulb and we'd all freeze our tails off.

You might die next week, tomorrow — or five seconds from now. You could seize up in cardiac arrest *as you read this very sentence.*

Most of us navigate our lives as if death were the North Star, a fixed and distant point. We're correct that life ending is a "fixed" certainty. We're wrong, however, to navigate by the assumption that it is far in the distance. We build our entire lives on the wildly presumptuous notion that death is far away and that we'll get to live to all eighty-seven years of statistical life expectancy.

We think we have time, so it's no surprise we postpone enjoying life until reaching some nebulous future date or state: after we graduate, get promoted, get married, have kids, lose weight, have enough money, retire, when we finally have time, when every other star in life is perfectly aligned and a fairy comes along to bop you on the head with her wand and tell you everything is perfect and now it's finally time to live how you want to live. *Then* we'll travel, then we'll write the book, then we'll spend quality time with the kids and grandkids, then we'll pause to mindfully sip tea on the porch.

Perplexingly, we expend a significant quantity of our Life Time rushing toward the societal milestones we believe will allow us to enjoy life in the future — all the while squandering the time we have in the palms of our hands to do so now.

I call it "Life Time" instead of "lifetime" for a reason. A "lifetime" is defined as the duration of a person's life. It's the block of time we are alive. Life Time, however, refers to your active resource of alive time. Your Life Time is every moment that you are alive, breathing, feeling, loving, making choices. Your Life Time is your active resource, rather than a passive unit of time only measurable in retrospect. Lifetime...even the word seems to conjure a long road stretching off into the mountains. While our lifetime may be a long road, our Life Time is akin to a raindrop which, just as quickly as it lands, rolls off and evaporates.

Death is paradoxical: an unknown certainty. It is one hundred percent certain that we will die, but zero percent certain as to when. It is one hundred percent certain, however, that our "when" *could be tomorrow.* To live as if the timing of our death is as fixed and far as the North Star is to plot one's life on a timeline made of sand.

We're better off imagining life as a shooting star: a varying, unknown, and often brief existence. Some shooting stars flash so briefly you may wonder if you even saw it at all. Others sear brightly across the sky for two or three seconds. We're unsure what exactly is out there and how far it goes, but we know that meteors flash and crash. Stars burn out. Like everything in our universe, we die. All we know is that everything is impermanent.

Like Charles Bukowski says, most of us don't prepare at all for death — our own or others' — and are terribly shocked when it happens. Bukowski suggests we'd be better off to keep death in our left pocket and pull it out every now and then to say, "Hey you, how ya doin'?" and let it know we'll be ready.

Not thinking about your death does not make it go away. Death is a universal human certainty, not yet controlled by science or government. You might not "beat cancer." You might not blow out next year's birthday candles. You might not make it to your destination next time you get into the car.

The potential scarcity of life begets its value. Think of it in terms of supply and demand. When demand for a good or service is high, but the supply is low, consumers will pay more. Think, for example, of infamous American holiday toy-buying frenzies for products like Tickle Me Elmo or Furby. Demand was high; people rushed to buy the toy, often literally trampling one another in the pursuit. It sells out, and the trampled, empty-handed individuals headed to alternate sales channels like eBay and paid multiple times the selling price to obtain the out-of-stock item. This is a good metaphor for life, except that in life, we often don't realize how badly we want to really live until it is already just about sold out. If only we would seek to live with the same desperation of those who sought the scarce Furby.

Psychologically, scarcity causes tunnel vision. As an adaptive survival measure, a person affected by the scarcity of a basic need like food, shelter, water, or love has trouble focusing on anything but satisfying their need for that necessity.

A scarcity mindset in the context of life and time — resources that are unable to be re-acquired once lost — benefits us in the same manner. In a world full of distractions and competing priorities, that we die elevates the value of living.

But a mortal mindset, one that acknowledges the potential scarcity of life, is not without challenges. A conversation about death is not complete without acknowledging fear.

Although death is fixed, one's attitude toward it is malleable. I see three common responses to accepting the reality of mortality:

apathy, anxiety, or productive action. In apathy, one chooses to take a perspective of nihilism, that everything in life is meaningless. An individual living anxiously in the face of mortality expends great energy worrying about death and attempting to fend it off, likely resulting in a life so consumed with avoiding death that the experience of living is stunted. In the third option, one chooses to respond to the unknown certainty of death by zealously and urgently consuming the resource of life while it lasts. That is, to profoundly love life while accepting that it will one day end.

As the one universal human fear, death is inherently scary to a degree. It is impossible to completely eradicate our fear of death. Even the Buddha said, "All tremble at violence; all fear death." What we can do productively is use that fear to our advantage.

Fear makes people move; discomfort begets action. If we live with the goal of minimizing this fear, it conveniently becomes self-diminishing.

While we cannot overcome the fear of death, we can overcome the terror of death. The fire of phobia and dread can be reduced to a low burn, and with the available energy we can create a vibrant life for ourselves. Our fear of death is, in large part, a fear of not living before we die. We have limited time and energy in life. It can be expended fearing or trying to circumvent dying, or it can be spent living with urgency, joy, and meaning. You make your choice with every action you take, great and small.

It's easy to get caught up in the washing machine of life. There is and will always be a hailstorm of insignificant problems, annoyances, and distractions — what people think of you, scheduling your next dentist appointment, how you will make money, the news, what you think you should do to please others —and they all fight to take your time and attention. If you pay too much attention to them, though, they make you forget that it's your one life, and you can do whatever the hell you want with it.

That we die is actually life's most beautiful gift: it's a portal to perspective in a chaotic world, it gives us a reason to appreciate being alive, and it reminds us that we have no time to waste. It minimizes the bullshit we so often allow ourselves to get caught up in. Awareness that we die and we don't know when can cultivate feelings of gratitude and awe for the wonder of being alive. Thinking about death reminds us that we're not yet dead. And everyone alive has access to it — it's free.

People who are actively dying from a terminal illness or who have had a near-death experience are the populations most likely to experience the radical insight and transformation offered by mortality awareness. But how unfortunate to wait to appreciate and enjoy life until death is at hand?

If you live a good life, you prepare yourself for a good death. If really living is the best way to diminish one's fear of dying, you must first clarify what it means to you to really live. In the absence of a universal meaning of life, you must create your own.

If you were to die right now, how would you feel about the state of your life? What have you left undone, unsaid? What, or who, are you most grateful for? Do they know this? Have you done anything you're still proud of now that societal ideals mean nothing? Do you wish you had not lived your life hiding your true self? Did you give yourself a chance to live for yourself? The next page is intentionally left blank for you to write down your gut response.

So, what happened? Did you write something down? What crossed your mind, your heart? What did you feel in your gut?

Most likely, you bought this book because you want to wake up. You want to have a frank conversation about your mortality, pull it out of the darkness and into the light. You want to quell your fears and anxieties about dying by looking them in the face. You want to find the spark, the joy of life. You are tired of trying to control everything, or of feeling that you have no control over your own life. You're sick of being in decision paralysis and want to find the motivation to do the meaningful things you want to do — before it's too late. You're tired of living the same year over and over again and calling it a life. You're terrified of waking up on your eighty-fifth birthday in declining health and realizing you're no longer capable or have the time to do the things you wanted to do. You want your experience near the end of life to be one of contentment and gratitude for a life well-lived. You want to live life *alive* — and in alignment with your soul's meaning.

You need to remember you are going to die in order to actually live.

In this book, I am your Tyler Durden, Palahniuk's character who reminds us, "This is your life and it's ending one moment at a time." I do not care if you like me. I am not impressed by how much money you have, or the bullshit lies you allow your ego to tell yourself in order to stay afloat. Trust me — I know. I tell myself the same ones. The ego is cunning and seemingly omnipotent, but mortality puts it all into perspective.

I have to be blunt because I'm here to help you see that death offers a perspective on life like nothing else can. It strips away the insignificant worries and exposes the thieves of time we allow to consume our lives. What we are left with is of minute quantity but, if we are doing it at all right, of great volume. Love. Family (also love). Joy (love of life). Benevolence (also love). Did I mention love?

I won't ask you to skydive if you don't want to, or quit your job if you don't want to, or forgive your mom if you don't want to (but let the record show that adventure, calculated risk, and forgiveness make for a really badass life). What I'm asking you to do is to get cozy with the notion of your mortality and the fears it brings up so you can experience the truth it brings to your life. I want you to feel the same fire for life that I have felt since I put my arm around death's shoulders and began walking arm in arm with it.

You have time *now* to prepare for your good death by living your good life. Let's get started.

Life.*

*Available for a limited time only. Limit one (1) per person. Subject to change without notice. Provided "as is" and without any warranties. Nontransferable and is the sole responsibility of the recipient. May incur damages arising from use or misuse. Additional parts sold separately. Your mileage may vary. Subject to all applicable fees and taxes. Terms and conditions apply. Other restrictions apply.

—Unknown

PART I:

LEARN FROM MY RADICAL AWAKENING

□

CHAPTER 1:

FOLLOWING THE BLUEPRINT

As young girls, my sister and I read a young adult novel called *A Time for Dancing*. It's about two teenaged best friends and their experiences after one of them is diagnosed with leukemia. I cried a waterfall the first time I read it and every time thereafter. My sister and I still treasure it to this day. We were so affected because it was the first time we were confronted with the picture of a young, vibrant person devolving into a frail, sick person and ultimately dying. Later, as a freshman at a small Catholic high school, that picture came to life. Carrie, a senior I did not know personally, became gravely ill with a rare form of cancer. Watching her health deteriorate affected me and most everyone at the school.

On the day of the school choir group's performance — the group she had been a key member of and was now too frail to stand and sing with — her family brought her to the cathedral on a stretcher to watch. She lay in the middle of the church on a bed of white sheets and fluffy pillows, wearing her blonde wig. I looked down on her with curiosity from the loft above. She was only seventeen, and though her body looked like that of a ninety-year-old woman's, she beamed with pride and joy as she took in the concert. She died soon after.

A few months later, Chester killed himself. Chester was a sophomore who was great at sports and making people laugh.

Everyone knew him, if not for his antics at school, then for his all-star performance on the sports fields.

I happened to be one of the last people to talk to him. My memory of the scene is crystal clear, like a movie I can turn on in my mind at any moment. Sunny, normal high school day by all accounts; a good day, even. School had just let out, and Chester and I were walking from hallways opposite each other, both heading toward the vestibule of the front doors. He's holding a bag of ice to his groin. He looks at me with an enormous goofy grin and asks, "Want to ice my balls?" I laugh and shake my head at him as we pass.

A few hours later, he hanged himself in his basement.

I experienced real grief for the first time. To process my emotions, I made Chester a mix CD and drove around aimlessly for hours, listening to it on repeat. I dealt with the range of feelings that come with grief: confusion, anger, intense sadness, apathy, and numbness. At Chester's funeral, his family spoke of his bipolar disorder. I cognitively understood that explanation, but it did not quell my struggle to understand *why*. We expected Carrie's death: she was very sick, and we saw her decline over time. Chester's death was like a hard slap to the face: jarring, unexpected, and very painful.

Why would someone take their own life? How could someone who seemed so happy be so desperate and sad inside? Could I have done something to prevent it? How will his family ever recover? How will I process this grief?

And for the first time in my life, I considered my own mortality. I felt myself grip life a little more tightly. *I don't want to die. I'm fifteen. I want to live.*

As it goes, life pressed on. Time began to heal the wounds. I thought of Chester often but, eventually, looked back on the experience as an isolated incident and a lesson that depression and suicide aren't just an affliction of the outwardly sad.

Then, my junior year of high school, I moved from Iowa to San Diego. Try, just *try*, to get sympathy from your friends in Iowa when you tell them you are moving away to Southern California.

Growing up, I had always said I was a California girl, despite never having set foot in the state. It turned out to be true. In San Diego, I hit my stride. Moving to California was one of the best things to ever happen to me. I loved the beach so much that I only applied to colleges on the coast.

In the end, however, I ended up declining my few university acceptance letters in favor of following my high school boyfriend to Santa Barbara to attend Santa Barbara City College. Adam, I've got to thank you for this one. You saved me thousands of dollars in tuition and led me to my now-favorite American city. In case you haven't been, let me describe it. Santa Barbara is paradise. It smells like flowers, the streets are picture-perfect, beaches plentiful, the farmer's market the most varied and vibrant I've experienced, the people dress like they've stepped off the pages of a magazine, and the restaurants are fantastic. If it's good enough for Oprah, it's good enough for me.

For as many stupid things as all my friends and I did in college (and I mean stupid — I was in handcuffs for party-related crimes just shy of the number of fingers on my left hand), I and everyone I knew lived. Death was not a thought in my mind. I was having the time of my life — partying, studying, dating (Adam and I eventually broke up), going to the beach. After I completed my general education credits, I transferred to the University of California in Santa Barbara and relished the reading I was assigned as a literature major. I was on such a life high that I ended up getting married while I was still in college — at twenty-one, to a different guy than the one I had followed there.

Jardel and I were introduced by my best friend Caroline. He was stop-in-the-street gorgeous: tan and muscular with soft, dark brown eyes; full, beautiful lips; and a smile that lit up his face. The night we met, we stayed up "talking" all night long. I use the quotes because we didn't actually talk much: he didn't speak any English. So mostly he said things in Portuguese, I swooned, we made out, got semi-naked on the couch, I swooned some more, and then the sun came up and we went to breakfast.

Before we parted ways that morning, we had a lightning bolt moment in which we looked at each other and the earth felt like it stood still. Our entire future together was illuminated in my consciousness and a shockwave of knowing went through my soul that this person was The One. I will never forget that moment for as long as I live.

As I got to know him better, I loved his confidence, his charisma, and the way his strong arms wrapped around me. I loved the fact that he was four years older and wiser. I was impressed that he had had the courage to leave an unfulfilling career as a criminal lawyer in Brazil to travel to an unknown country. And if I'm honest, I loved that he was *from* another country. Early in our relationship, I insatiably consumed knowledge and experiences of Brazilian culture and Portuguese language. It was the kind of love that makes you do crazy things.

The way I felt is perfectly described by my adventure idol Dan Fredinburg in his answer to the question, "What is the greatest risk you have ever taken?"

"While climbing Carstensz Pyramid, the tallest mountain in Oceania, a fellow climber fell, lost a lot of her blood, and nearly died of hypothermia. Had we returned on the 6-day trek through the jungle that we used on the way in, she would have certainly died. To rescue her, I smuggled her through Grasberg Mine, the largest gold mine in the world. Along the way, we risked being shot by mercenaries, had our friends kidnapped and held hostage, and then were ultimately arrested and imprisoned inside a jail inside the gold mine. And I was on Mt Everest this year...when an ice serac fell into the icefall and killed sixteen sherpas on the mountain. Afterwards we executed body recovery and then climbed back down through the damaged route.

But these were mostly calculated risks.

If I had to select the greatest risk I've taken in my life, it has been to throw myself into a romantic relationship with someone to reach a point of deep, illogical and visceral love. To a point where emotion and human connection overpowers any reason and safety. To be vulnerable psychologically and emotionally. This is real risk, with the greatest reward."

Deep in that illogical state of love, less than one year after that lightning bolt moment, we eloped. Out on the lushly green and flowered grounds of the Santa Barbara courthouse, the officiant's husband served as our single witness. Nope, we didn't invite a single friend or family member. In the beautiful and all-encompassing haze of love, and with the urgency created by his foreign status, we got married as soon as possible. We called our parents after the ceremony and told them the news. As you can imagine, they were not exactly...celebratory. We attempted to ease the blow by emphatically promising them we would eventually have a 'real' family wedding to which they would be invited.

After that, life went on. I graduated college, we visited his family in Brazil every other year, we got a dog. Eventually, we followed my parents to Austin, where I got a job in marketing at Google and we bought a house.

I thought I had checked off the right boxes: I was married, had a dog, a house, and a job. It seemed like my adult life had been tied up in a lovely bow. I thought this meant I could live happily ever after.

CHAPTER 2:

DECISION PARALYSIS

It's 2014, and I'm enormous. I had discovered that the secret antidote to anguish is eating mashed potatoes. I knew deep down that I had to get out of this marriage, but I. Just. Can't. Do. It. Trapped in decision paralysis, I found that the only time I wasn't gripped with anxiety and dread was when I was chewing. So, like a cow, I chewed slowly and often. Quite often. Twenty pounds often.

I could eat all the potatoes I wanted (and trust me, I did), but I was only numbing myself against the truth I knew deep inside. Our marriage had devolved from young, blinding love to an insurmountable mountain of rejection and hurt. Neither of us knew how to communicate and almost always defaulted to shutting one another out. After a fight, it was not unusual for us to go two weeks without talking. Eventually, we would resume communication, but never about the issue at hand. The cycle would repeat over and over again, with pain, resentment, and distance building each time around. Our marriage had diverged into two independently led lives. We were both alone yet deeply hurt by not being met by the other person. When the blissful high from those delicious, comforting carbohydrates wore off, and the bowl was empty, I was back to my painful reality.

I came up with every excuse in the book not to leave my

unhappy marriage: *I don't have the money to live on my own. We used to be so in love! If I can't make this marriage work, I'm a failure. He is so good looking; I'll never get anyone that attractive again. What will our families think? I think he is depressed, if I leave him now that would be a cruel violation of the whole 'in sickness' clause that we signed…twice.*

Yes, this marriage that I now needed to get out of so badly, I had consciously and enthusiastically (and legally) consented to on not one, but two occasions. That's two weddings.

To make a short story long, four years after that courthouse quickie, his whole family announced they were coming to visit us in America for the first time since we met. I was ecstatic! The whole which-country-to-have-the-wedding-in quandary was solved! I announced that we would have a real live wedding with the whole fam-damily while they were here. The short version is that we never should have married the second time around.

So you see, I consciously suggested, orchestrated, and completed two marriages to this man, and now, just one year after this church, white dress, friends and family second wedding, I had spiraled into deep, soul-crushing doubt about whether I should be married to my husband. In my 'completely honest with myself' version of the story, it wasn't doubt. For those three years I spent hurting and in agonizing indecision and all the while I ate large quantities of potatoes and drank bottles of wine like they were cans of Diet Coke, I knew all along I should leave. I just chose to ignore it with every fiber of my being.

Imagine agonizing about a single decision for three years. No, not whether to mash or twice bake. Something seemingly so big and undecidable that for the better part of 1,095 days you drive yourself crazy going back and forth — not like an eager first-grader on a playground swing, but like the tortuous swing of a pendulum on a loud, ticking clock while you're waiting to find out whether or not you'll be sentenced to death.

I was paralyzed in indecision in the heaviest, most agonizing situation of my life up to that point. But I had no idea what was to come next.

June

It started with an unexpected call on a Saturday morning from my dear friend and fellow Google colleague, Cody.

"Morning, Cody!" I said cheerfully. It was a beautiful day outside and Cody always had the best impromptu weekend invitations.

"Hi," he began. "Are you sitting down?"

"Yes, I am now." My words came out in a playful drawl. I was looking forward to what he had in store.

"I heard something — could be a rumor — that Stephen… Stephen drowned." I felt a pop of electricity run through my body, and I leapt to my feet.

"What? WHAT? Is he ok? He's not even in town right now."

"He's not ok. AJ called me a few minutes ago. He got an email from the guys who were with him on the trip." Cody's tone was soft and empathetic, but he spoke with purpose. I was frozen erect and speechless.

"They were kayaking," he continued, "and came upon a cliff. Stephen climbed up and jumped, and…he didn't come back up. They looked for him and the emergency people came, but they…haven't actually found his body yet. It's been almost twenty-four hours."

"Oh my God, Cody." I felt the gravity of the situation press in on my chest. I looked desperately around my bedroom as if to confirm I was in reality. It felt as if I, and everything around me, had frozen.

"What do we do, Cody? How do we find out if it's true?"

"I think it is true, Kate. And I think you should call his manager to let him know."

We hung up, and I knew I had to do what Cody had asked. Stephen was my manager. I needed to notify *his* boss. I gathered up the strength to make the call to Stephen's boss. I relayed to him what I had heard, and he shakily replied in disbelief that it couldn't be true. He hung up to get in touch with Stephen's family.

He called me back an hour later to let me know that it was true.

Stephen Carney, my kooky, cocky, triathlete, benevolent, energetic manager, was dead at 27 from a cliff diving accident while on vacation. The news soon broke publicly, and I compulsively refreshed my Google search of his name for two days until the articles were updated to say they had finally found his body, 800 feet downstream. I wailed aloud in grief for the reality and finality of it.

The news agencies stated that Stephen had been the first to scramble up the thirty-foot cliff to show off his front-flip, and that he had probably over-rotated and hit the water at a bad angle, potentially exacerbated by high waters with debris from recent flooding. They used his LinkedIn photo in their coverage, a photo

I had taken of Stephen just a few weeks before. This very, very alive person, who I had spent every Monday through Friday with for the past year, would never show up to work again.

His memorial service was aptly held at a stunt ranch and concluded with an epic firework display to celebrate the life of the vivacious man who had been born on the Fourth of July.

Back at work, it was obvious that everyone on our team was deeply shaken by the sudden death of a person we knew so well, and who was around our same age. For weeks afterward, we struggled to find some normalcy at work. Soon, we just stopped talking about it. Awkward moments, heavy with unspoken feelings, became the norm. Eventually, one of my peers was promoted to take Stephen's place as my manager. Work and life went on as if nothing had happened. I began spending nights reading the messages on his Facebook page and sending notes to his inbox. I suffered in silence, like I'm sure many of my teammates did.

Stephen's death brought back the intense feelings I had when Chester committed suicide in high school. I was again shocked by the idea that I or other young people could die. I felt confused and afraid of this reality. Death, only recently barely a blip on my radar since high school, had again become very, very real.

October

Ivan was Jardel's cousin, older by a few years. I had grown close with him during my many visits to Brazil and when he stayed with us for a couple of weeks on his solo trip around California. A Great Dane of a man, physically huge but with a soft heart, he was diagnosed with renal cancer at 35 years old. Jardel and his tight-knit family struggled with the grave diagnosis, and they remained convinced he would survive, even after the cancer metastasized to his lungs. Finally, the reality of the situation began to set in. Jardel flew to Brazil to see Ivan one last time. His body was ravaged by the disease. Six months after his diagnosis, just after his 36th birthday and only four months after Stephen's death, Ivan died in the hospital. Jardel was there with him, having arrived at his bedside two days before.

That day, I was touring Inside Outside School for a work project with Nirvan Mullick, the creator of the YouTube sensation *Caine's Arcade*. Inside Outside School is this remarkable alternative elementary school in an old residential farmhouse on a big plot of land just outside Austin city limits. The former bedrooms of the house function as classrooms, but much of the instruction occurs outside on the school's property. The children go on nature walks, garden, meditate, do science experiments in the creek, and take care of the chickens and goats.

As we walked up to the large animal pen, I looked on with wonder as baby pygmy goats galloped and skipped around. Yes, you read that correctly: *baby pygmy goats*. Like regular goats but five hundred times cuter. When the principal asked if I'd like to go in and spend time with the goats, I shrieked with glee and scurried into the pen.

Seated on a log, I was soon covered by these fairy tale creatures. The goats ranged in size from that of a small bunny to about the size of a Jack Russel terrier, some replete with beards and tiny horns. They nuzzled my shirt and chomped on my hair. As I took my phone out to record a video, I received the message: Ivan had died.

Tears sprang to my eyes as I felt the loss of burly, smiling, bass-playing Ivan. I put down my phone and placed my hands on the beautiful brown goat upon my lap. I let him chew my hair as I stroked his side and imagined Ivan's soul going up into heaven or the universe or someplace beautiful, without any more pain. I decided I would not share the news with Nirvan or our tour guides or run immediately back home. Home was empty, anyway — Jardel was in Brazil. I had nowhere to be other than exactly where I was: outside in nature, covered in pygmy goats.

I closed my eyes and felt the moment entirely: I heard the birds in the trees, the gentle sounds of the creek, the occasional bleat, and the crackle of leaves and stones as the goats scampered around their pen. I felt the air surrounding me and the coarse yet somehow silky goat fur under my fingers. The serendipitous beauty being out in nature and 'attacked' by tiny, sweet creatures was juxtaposed with my profound sadness that Ivan was no longer in this world after such a short life. I somehow felt more alive as my grief welled up inside of me. Tears escaped my eyes as I felt it all. A few moments later, as we all stood to conclude the tour, I caught sight of a goat clacking his heels together as he sailed high over a log. I smiled.

Jardel and I had been having intense relationship struggles for two years, with lots of silence, hurt, and resentment between us. When he returned from Brazil after Ivan's death, it was like he was a different person — and we, a different couple. He was suddenly loving, attentive, and sweet. When I asked him about the change, he said he saw so clearly now that life is short and unfair, but that family is the most important part. I felt a glimmer of hope that this new perspective from death might give us a chance to overcome our past hurt and resentment. For a couple of months after Ivan's death, the great wall between us was broken down.

Although we were kinder to each other, as with Stephen, we suffered our grief in private. Neither Jardel nor I had the courage to open up to one another about the pain and sadness we were both feeling. I failed to reach out to him in the way he needed to be comforted as he grieved the loss of his cousin. Instead of being a leader and persistent in my attempts to comfort him, after a few far-too-gentle attempts, I slipped into my own darkness, spending nights reading Ivan's old blog and watching his band's videos on YouTube, crying.

I began to believe that my body was filled with cancer-causing toxins and would go on two- and three-week cleanse diets to purge them. Death and grief, though unacknowledged, were now present both at work and at home, and I felt alone in my grief and terror. The great wall between my husband and I went back up, brick by emotionally-desperate-but-unable-or-unwilling brick. I didn't know how to talk to Jardel about how I felt or know how to comfort him. I worried increasingly that he, too, would die unexpectedly. Death was now very much in my life and presented as a mysterious force that could strike at any moment. I felt a growing part of my energy consumed by avoiding it and also mentally preparing for it. Stephen had died in a freak accident at 27; Ivan died from aggressive cancer at 36. I was only 28 — would I be next?

December

I stopped cold in my Facebook scrolling when I saw the post: Mallory was hit by a drunk driver as she walked with friends across Anacapa Street in Santa Barbara. The driver slowed to see what he had hit, then sped off, until he hit a tree and was caught. Mallory was rushed to the hospital, her brain and body gravely injured, but alive.

My life had been intertwined with Mallory's for several years: we went to college at UCSB together, were neighbors in Isla Vista, and worked together in a tight-knit crew at a popular bar. I had been jealous of her in our work and social lives. Mallory was the life of the party, and while I tried to be a part of the 'cool' friend group among the bar employees, Mallory *was* the friend group. She was loud and blunt yet cute and funny and always the ringleader of every mischievous prank and party plan. I would venture a guess that every person who worked in any bar on State Street knew Mallory and had enjoyed a drink with her and her raucous energy.

I compulsively and obsessively read updates and news and social updates about the incident and her condition. For days, she lay in the Intensive Care Unit, unconscious with severe brain trauma. The community came together for Mallory in the days following the accident. The waiting room at Cottage Hospital overflowed with people who came to support her. They made signs and erected tributes outside the hospital and at the location where she was hit. Her friends created VOW4MAL, an activism movement against drunk driving, which was a serious problem in nightclub-choked, wine-soaked Santa Barbara. The outpouring of love for Mallory impressed me and, as she had in college, made me a bit jealous of her. I couldn't help but wonder: If this had happened to me, would there be the same outpouring of love and support? I was doubtful.

I continued my obsessive monitoring of her fragile status between life and death. En route to Atlanta for a business trip, I turned my phone back on after landing and immediately went to her medical updates webpage. After five days of tests, surgeries, and hopeful watching and waiting for any glimmer of life or improvement, the doctors had let Mallory's parents know that she had no chance of recovering from the brain trauma. Her mom and dad made the decision to take her off life support. All around me, people on my flight began getting up and getting their bags, but I just sat in my seat with tears streaming down my face. It was all over; she was gone forever. I ached for her short life and cried away the hope to which I had been clutching tightly over the past five days.

After the rush of passengers disembarked, I stood up and ambled out of the plane. At the end of the jetway, my tears dried up. I felt a darkness come over me. I sat down in the empty bank of seats near the gate to process.

Mallory was dead. It had been six months since Stephen died and just two months since Ivan died. I realized I could die at any moment, on vacation like Stephen, from an unexpected cancer diagnosis like Ivan, or even just crossing the goddamn street like Mallory. Tragedy after tragedy — who was safe? I was 28 years old, and always thought I had 50 more years to live. My sense of safety in life had disappeared.

Hi, My Name is Anxiety. It's Nice to Meet You.

For three years, I had been trapped by my indecision in a marriage that made me feel isolated and ate away my sense of self-worth. And now, after three rapid-fire young fatalities, my sense of security about staying alive was obliterated.

I became plagued with visions of dying, particularly when I was driving. I'd drive through an intersection and vividly envision getting T-boned by a speeding car. On an overpass, I would grip the steering wheel tightly, thinking about losing control and going over the edge. I would anxiously wonder if I had hit someone back at that intersection and whether they were still under the car.

I'd go down long thought paths thinking about my own death. I'd get so deep into these visions that I'd imagine the complex succession of events after I died: how people would find out, who *wouldn't* find out at all, who would come to my funeral, how my stuff would be divided up. About how my mom would slide into a deep depression and my sister would feel like a part of her had died, too.

I also had persistent, uncontrollable visions of people I loved dying. As I lay in bed alone at night, the scenario of Jardel not returning home would snap into my mind, and I couldn't push it out. I would imagine the call I would get and then calling his family and telling them the news. I would see myself on the long flight to Brazil for his funeral, and I'd weigh whether I would be a complete mess or a stoic survivor under the circumstances. These scenes in my head felt so real that I would have visceral reactions: I felt the weight of his death in my chest and sobs would often bubble up out of me.

Eventually, I was gripped by death anxiety and depression all the time — save for those moments of relief when I was focused on the act of chewing. The terror of death haunted every corner, in every sweet aspect of my life, and every roadway intersection I crossed. Soon, I couldn't sleep at night because I couldn't shut off the movies in my head which rolled on mercilessly. The sound of the phone ringing unexpectedly would send me into a panic attack.

I couldn't take it anymore. I found a therapist who specialized in loss.

Dr. Balasingham was not the first therapist I had seen, but she was the first I had opened up to so fully. I hadn't confided in anyone about the potential death of my marriage and feelings of being shut out emotionally, what I was feeling about the deaths in my life, or my debilitating death anxiety. I had kept it inside so as not to burden those around me, so when I sat down in front of an impartial audience who was legally bound to keep my secrets, everything flowed out of me like rosé on a Sunday in Manhattan.

Like a waterfall, I talked, cried, and released as I had never done before in my life. I told her everything, including about my mashed potatoes and red wine coping mechanisms. I'd come into her office beating myself to hell after a night of polishing off a bottle of red and grams of carbs in the triple digits, and she'd say, "Well, Kate, maybe that's what you need right now. Trust that you won't let it get out of control."

At first, I thought I had somehow won the doctor lottery by finding the one who says it's okay to find self-actualization through wine and mashed potatoes. Dr. Balasingham, however, had a bigger plan. Instead of sending me to the nearest rehab, my clever therapist worked to take me out of the cycle where one bad day turned into four bad days because I felt guilty about wallowing on the first bad day — simply by teaching me to be compassionate with myself. I began to picture her in a Monet painting, because she was soft, and she taught me to be soft with myself. My Monet doctor gave me the incredible, unexpected gifts of self-compassion and space to feel.

I had learned how to be kinder to myself and actually feel emotion, but I was still paralyzed in my life. I was paralyzed by the fear of death and by the difficult decision of whether to leave my marriage. Outside therapy, I was still completely reactive to my emotions and experiences.

Part of decision paralysis, I learned, is a hope — whether conscious or subconscious — that while the paralyzed individual waits it out, the situation will change itself as a result of external forces. The benefit of this? The passive turn of events thereby relieves oneself of the burden of the decision and its consequences. The disadvantage? Not having the experience or pride of actively creating one's ideal life.

After more than three years of agonizing indecision, I hit the passive version of the decision paralysis jackpot: I learned my husband had been seeing another woman for a couple of months. To this day, I still believe that God and/or the Universe (whatever you call your greater power, or if you're an atheist, just go with me) somehow caused him to start seeing her so that we could finally have a concrete reason to walk away from one another. Getting "cheated on" is, and probably always will be, one of the events in my life for which I am most grateful. I had my out, and this time, I wasn't going to let the cycle of indecision begin again. I printed and signed the divorce papers that night and filed at the court-house the next morning. Because when you get even a glimmer, a tiny speck, a soft whisper of clarity, YOU MUST ACT NOW.

* * *

In the year following our divorce as we started our separate lives, I moved to the 'cool' part of Austin and got my first solo apartment, continued working at my job that I enjoyed, and started living the single life for the first time since I was 20 years old. I was finding my footing in my new life, learning and growing. I don't remember much specifically from that time, other than it being the first time in years that I was able to live without being overwhelmed and heavy with emotional pain and struggle.

When the smoke cleared, however, I found myself only back to zero. While I had gotten out of a relationship that no longer served me and started fresh, all my other dissatisfactions and shortcomings did not disappear as a result (surprise!). I was no longer in active agony about my marriage, and my death anxiety had subsided by half, but when the novelty of my new life wore off, I looked around and found myself feeling numb, apathetic, and unfulfilled. I was still the same decision-averse Kate with no urgency to live or sense of autonomy over my life. I was like a dandelion seed in my own life, pushed this way and that by the winds of external forces.

But deep down, I did know what I wanted. I had always dreamed of traveling to places so different from what I knew that my head would spin. I wanted to connect with other humans, talk to them, see firsthand how they lived their lives. I wanted to break open my mind with new perspectives and ways of life. Marrying a Brazilian turned out to be a wonderful and privileged way to accomplish exactly that. But I wanted to know more than just Brazil.

Outside of our trips to Brazil, we rarely traveled together. For years I had made it known that I wanted us to take a trip together, but traveling was not a priority or a dream for Jardel at that time in his life.

After seven years of hoping he would change his mind, in the first year of the three years of relationship decision paralysis, I decided to make it happen for myself. I got my first travel credit card and saved up the miles I earned for months until I had enough for a round trip international flight. I traveled to Italy alone and then flew to Santorini to meet one of my oldest and dearest friends, Margeaux.

Traveling alone felt so natural to me. I sipped wine at a small table in a piazza in Venice, solved my way out of a missed a five AM train to Florence, and relished the countryside town of Cortona. I walked up and down the rows of grapes in the sunny vineyards, singing joyfully to myself and the vines.

A whole year free from the relationship that "held me back" from traveling, I still hadn't taken another trip. In fact, for that entire period after my divorce, my best friend Melissa repeatedly invited me to visit her in Tahiti, where she and her husband lived on their sailboat. I declined each invitation, citing an array of excuses. In truth, I had little reason not to go — I mean, really, free lodging in Tahiti! — but I again chose inaction. It would appear obvious now who was holding me back from traveling, wouldn't it? I had all the freedom in the world, and yet I was a weak participant in my life, feeling uninspired, listless, and bored yet afraid of living and assuming there would always be more time to get around to it.

CHAPTER 3:
A DIE/DIE SITUATION

This next part of the story is about a guy I met once. Remember that beautiful quote earlier in the book about a person who had smuggled his gravely injured friend through a mine to safety and survived an icefall on Everest, but found love to be the greatest risk of all? It's the guy who wrote that: Dan Fredinburg.

I met him at a fancy bar in San Francisco during a work party in 2012. We were introduced that night by his good friend and my team lead at the time, Max. Dan and I talked for maybe fifteen minutes, but in that short time, our conversation somehow included everything from what lit us up in life to us crafting Olympic gymnast names for one another. Not a word was spoken about work, so I figured he was a friend of Max's who had tagged along. Though brief, the interaction stuck with me: it was a funny and unusually genuine first conversation. It didn't hurt that he was also tall, with sparkling eyes and a bright smile.

A few days later, he requested to connect with me on social media, and from there, I began my fandom of his life. I learned that he did, in fact, work at Google — as the Head of Privacy for Google X. On the side, he climbed mountains, sometimes with a 360-degree camera on his back for Google Street View. He mapped the route to Everest Base Camp for Google in 2011. I found Dan to be gorgeous, inspired, driven, funny, and since I met him in person, very real.

Over the span of three years, I watched through a computer screen as he dated a celebrity, opened a coworking and idea incubation space, and attempted to summit Mount Everest. Summiting Everest is very different than the trek to base camp. Getting to base camp is a comparatively leisurely hike that takes a little more than a week and has lovely tea houses to sleep at each night along the way. To reach the summit of the highest mountain peak in the world, it takes more than 40 days and includes scaling frozen waterfalls, climbing sheer rock faces and crevices, risk of avalanche, climbing falls, and potentially fatal altitude sickness — all in temperatures below freezing.

On Dan's first summit attempt, he was forced to turn back part way up because a deadly icefall killed sixteen sherpas in the group behind him one morning. He and his team executed body recovery. That harrowing experience did not stop him. I marveled as I watched him return home and begin training for his second attempt.

I wanted his vibrancy, his drive, his sense of adventure. Without ever having the courage or arrogance of belonging in life to reach out to him directly, I lived vicariously through his bright life and daring adventures. I, on the other hand, stayed on the straight and narrow of what I thought I was supposed to do in life, working in a big company, dating, shopping, watching television, and waiting for retirement. I felt a desire to live even a fraction of an adventurous life like Dan's, but I was too fearful to do anything about it. Instead, I watched this aspirational animal through pixels and fantasized about a life that wasn't mine.

I followed his Instagram updates, enraptured, as he attempted

Everest for the second time. He chronicled his experience training, arriving in Nepal, and his unbelievable journey all the way up to the mandatory altitude stop at Base Camp. I watched in awe as a person I had met in real life climbed the tallest mountain in the world. He was wielding an ice pick, for God's sake.

And then, Dan died.

I remember exactly where I was: I had just returned home to my sunny Austin apartment from a morning workout on a beautiful weekend day. I opened my phone to see what was happening in the world and saw the news headline: "Devastating Earthquake Strikes Nepal."

"No," I said aloud, my heart pumping with fear as I frantically pulled up Instagram to make sure Dan was okay.

A post on his page by his sister relayed the news. Dan had indeed died early that morning as a result of a head injury sustained in an avalanche triggered by the earthquake. My idol, my crush, my "kind of" friend, a bright light in my drab life, was dead. I curled up on my white sheets in my bright apartment and felt a vast, dark emptiness inside of me.

Soon, that emptiness turned into a very different emotion: rage. Again, I felt the solid ground of my existence ripped away as my mind ran through the deaths of all the young people I had experienced: Dan, Mallory, Ivan, Stephen, Carrie, Chester. Chester had committed suicide — but hadn't Dan also? Dan chose to engage in the very optional, very dangerous activity of climbing the tallest mountain in the world.

I sat bolt upright in bed, anger flickering through veins. My mind raced: *He had almost died the first time. He knew the risk in climbing that mountain, and he did it anyway. How could he do this to the world? He was so beautiful, so dynamic, his life such a bright light. Why? Why did he risk his life for adventure?*

Then, it hit me:

He *knew* he could die climbing that mountain, but had he not climbed it, he would not have truly lived.

My racing thoughts stopped short. Logic began to set in and go to work. Climbing Mount Everest isn't something you just do on a random Saturday. It takes great physical effort, investment of time and money, research, and detailed planning. For Dan, this was a calculated choice made with full awareness of the risk — and in alignment with the soul.

Attempting Everest was Dan's truth. It was a die/die situation: choose to climb and potentially die or choose to stay at sea level and not truly live.

My anger began to soften. My realizations forced me to look at my own life in contrast to Dan's. Here was this human radically and bravely living his truth, while I was consumed with anxiety about whether I would survive the four-way stop at Fifth Street. I realized I *could* die driving through an intersection, I could die climbing Everest, or I could die climbing the damn stairs. I have no control over when, where, or how I die, but I have complete control over how I live until that mystery moment comes.

I saw that I had spent vast quantities of time and energy in my life trying to excessively control whether I and the people around me would die unexpectedly. I saw how comical and ironic it was. Comical because I'm going to die no matter what, and ironic because in every other aspect of my life, I had been living like that floating dandelion seed, at the mercy of outside forces and phobic of making any choices at all. I was trying to control one of the only aspects of my life I could not.

My experiences of young mortality had shown me over and over again that life can end at any age. I had been terrified of this truth; all I wanted to do was avoid it at all costs. And the costs were huge. My fear of death had consumed me to the point that I was afraid to live.

It had never really crossed my mind, until then, that living is more than just existing. Life requires agency to be fully realized. Dan demonstrated that living authentically is worth risking life itself.

With the bright light of perspective shone on my life by Dan's death, the consuming anxiety that I might die tomorrow transmuted from a terrifying threat to a simple truth. An appreciation for death had been born. A great majority of my fear energy evaporated, and in its place, I was overcome with an intense zeal to *live while I am still alive*. I felt my energetic vibration rise up and out, and I felt so fucking happy to be alive.

I sat back on the bed and shook my head at the profound lesson Dan had imparted to me upon his death. He always said, "Adventure awaits." But what would my adventure be?

□

CHAPTER 4:

ADVENTURE AWAITS

After Dan's death, I felt I had been set on fire, more alive than ever in my life.

Life seemed to buzz through my veins. At random moments, like at stoplights or out getting the mail, I would be overwhelmed with a palpable sense of aliveness and immense gratitude for it. Everything in life seemed brighter and clearer, and I felt an urgency to do the things I had always wanted to do but had been putting off. I wanted adventure.

The first thing I did was finally take Melissa and Scott up on their long standing invitation for me to come visit them on their boat in Tahiti. By that time, they had been asking for a year and a half. For *a year and a half*, I declined an open door/open porthole invitation to stay on a houseboat in a tropical destination in the middle of the Pacific Ocean.

As I booked the flight, the many excuses I had given myself in that year and a half flickered back up in my mind: *Can I afford this? Do I even like sailing? Is this the best use of my vacation time from work? Will I be a bother to them?* I sternly ignored my bullshit excuses and fears and clicked "BOOK THIS FLIGHT." I no longer assumed I would have a future to take this trip. My fear had to take a back seat.

My new perspective also caused me to look at the reasons I had been feeling so empty. I had started dating after my divorce but found it to feel more disconnecting than exciting and fun. For the last several months, I had stayed in a "sort of" relationship with a much younger man who acted like he cared about me but wouldn't or couldn't verbalize it. I enjoyed nights out and live music with great friends, but I hadn't pursued an outlet for my creativity. I had a job that was fun, interesting, and paid well. Google's ethos taught me an impactful lesson: anyone has the power to change the world. It was one of the best things that ever happened to me, but I could see that I had built my self-worth around having a 'cool' job. I was that annoying person at the party who couldn't wait to be asked, "So, what do you do for work?" I could now see how hollow it was to feel like my job was my best defining characteristic as a human.

I wanted more. In truth, I wanted to be like Dan. Dan wasn't a Google employee who also had adventures, he was an adventurer who also happened to be a Google executive. Like Dan, I wanted to be epic, have epic experiences, and when I died, to be remembered as epic. I had the clarity now to see that I wanted more out of life, but I still wasn't quite sure what, exactly, I wanted to do.

In the weeks leading up to my Tahiti trip, people at work asked me about my upcoming vacation. I would half-jokingly reply that I was going to Tahiti to figure out my life.

Armed with an open mind and a soul on fire to experience life, I packed a bunch of bikinis and hopped on a plane to see my dear friend Melissa, learn what boat life was all about, and, apparently, to figure out my life.

My first idea came on the plane ride over. I was trying to think of ways to get out of nine to five life and create something that was my own. The idea? To open a potato-themed food truck. This should not be surprising to you, dear reader. You've already been made privy to my deep affinity for potatoes. Sure, I'm roughly half Irish, but my love for potatoes goes deeper than my genetic origins, all the way to my soul. I love potatoes in all forms and species, but I reach nirvana when I eat mashed potatoes. My delight in potatoes is well known in my family, and my mom makes an extra (okay, three extra) batches of mashed potatoes for me on all major holidays. One Christmas, I was caught hiding a spoon in my pocket for secret trips to the refrigerator during after-dinner card games. The next morning, it was discovered that I had eaten nearly a half-gallon of my drug of choice. I don't use the word 'drug' facetiously. I can actually feel high as I eat them, and once I start it's hard to stop. The carbs, the butter, the cream! Also, chives, which are critical in any good mashed potato recipe. It's pure comfort.

I started getting excited. This food truck idea would be something I could create to share my passion with others and make people feel good. I started planning my menu: perfectly crispy french fries fried in the best peanut oil, delicious mashed potatoes more comforting than a hug from your mom, loaded potato skins (a forgotten delicacy, in my opinion), and I could be the first person to bring the Brazilian-style hot dog to America. I bet you can guess what the Brazilians put on top of their hot dogs. Yep, a hearty scoop of white, fluffy mashed potatoes. Also, peas, but no need for pure authenticity here, folks. My food truck would be called Tater.

My flight connected in Los Angeles, where I linked up with Melissa's sister Shannon and their cousin, Elaine. Shannon and

Elaine had also never visited Melissa's floating home in the South Pacific, and we had all decided to join up for the trip.

We boarded the Air Tahiti Nui flight to Papeete, Tahiti, and seven hours later, we arrived and disembarked the plane onto the tarmac just before the sun rose. From what little we could see in the dark, we could have been arriving in sweaty Chicago pre-dawn, save for the ukulele and Tahitian dance trio serenading us as we walked from the plane to the gate. Melissa and Scott's boat wasn't actually on the island of Tahiti, though. They were anchored several islands away on Huahine, so we had one final flight to our destination.

None of us had ever traveled to such a remote place, so upon our arrival, some comical episodes ensued. We hadn't thought to learn any French, so due to confusion regarding our baggage overages for the tiny, weight-sensitive regional plane, we missed our scheduled interisland flight. Then, unprepared for the fact that our phones wouldn't work on a remote island, we had no way of notifying Melissa of our new flight. These all paled in comparison, however, to our realization once we arrived at the one-room airport hut in Huahine. We had no plan for how we would get from the airport on land to the actual boat — you know, *on the ocean.*

And then, Jocelyn arrived. A tall, strong woman with beach blonde hair, Jocelyn wore a loose sarong around her hips, a bright smile on her face, and she found us.

"Are you girls with Melissa? Come on. I'll take you over there."

We hoisted our luggage and ourselves into the back of her old Toyota pickup. As we rode out from the airport down a dirt road, we caught our first real glimpse of French Polynesia. I took in everything: velvet blue sky with fluffs of white clouds, lush greenery lining both sides of the road and beyond, the tall domed hills of the island. Everything was bright and clear, electric browns, greens, and blues. The air smelled like flowers. Perched on the edge of the bed of the pickup, I felt like such a badass.

My mouth dropped open when Jocelyn pulled up to the edge of the water. There, stretching as far as my eye could see, was the most stunning color of blue I had ever seen in my life. In front of that sparkling sea stood Melissa, beaming.

Melissa and I had been the closest of friends since I moved to San Diego in high school, where we were excellent troublemakers who lived for fun. She was the quintessential California girl: beautiful, athletic, and always up for an adventure. No one was surprised when she was selected to appear in a Discovery Channel survival reality show trekking remote Venezuela with no supplies, or when she was the only female to complete the challenge from a group of nine. Nor when she and her new boyfriend, Scott, decided to get a catamaran and sail from Hawaii to French Polynesia to start a new life living on the ocean. Despite knowing her adventurous history, it was surreal to see her here.

After excited hugs all around, she motioned toward a tiny metal and rubber dinghy bearing the haphazardly spray-painted name Animal. Shit was starting to get real, y'all. Animal was their tender to and from their houseboat. It had not entered my mind that her houseboat wouldn't be right there at the dock to pick us up. Somehow, we managed to get all humans and suitcases into the very unstable dinghy (because, you know, it's *floating*) and with that, Melissa fired up the outboard motor with ease. We sped away toward her houseboat, Kaimana.

Knowing something and seeing it for yourself are two completely different things. I'd seen on TV a million different lifestyles: people who work on crabbing ships, people who have twenty kids, athletes, actors, people who dedicate their lives to building their business empire. But even with all of these examples of different ways of life, it had never really occurred to me that I could do something besides go to college, get married, buy a house, get a dog, go shopping, work in an office, and maybe have kids. I hadn't ever considered *not* following the blueprint that I saw the people around me following.

All of that was about to change.

Kaimana came into view. We could see Scott standing at the edge of the blue and white catamaran jumping up and down with his fists pumping the air. I had never met him, but this was a fantastic start.

Somehow, in a flurry, we and all our luggage made it off the bobbing dinghy onto the main vessel. Melissa and Scott welcomed us with open arms and bestowed each of us with a shell necklace and another deep hug before showing us to the sleeping arrangements. I was shocked to see that the boat had four bedrooms with actual beds and bathrooms! My vision of boat sleeping arrangements had been canvas hammocks crowded in a single, dark under-vessel cavity. These rooms were light and bright with a stunning view; each had a side porthole facing the horizon and a window above the bed up to the deck. This was like an actual house.

After I dropped my suitcase in my cabin and changed into a bikini, I came up onto the deck. There I caught sight of Melissa and Scott, facing the water, each with an arm around the other. They stood proudly on their ship against the backdrop of that unbelievable cerulean sparkling water. It had taken them great drive, perseverance, and bravery to obtain Kaimana and sail her from California to Tahiti. I saw my friend now as she was: at home on this radical adventure at sea, living her most authentic expression of life.

That night, we went out to the lone bar on the island and ran into Melissa and Scott's Aussie friends. They were two guys and a girl, around 25 years old. The evening ended with us partying aboard the Aussie's epic sailboat. Melissa and Scott's catamaran was beautiful, yet practical (as practical as a shiny white four-cabin houseboat in Tahiti can be). The Aussie's sailboat was a floating mansion. I figured one of them must be a trust fund baby to afford a boat and lifestyle so extravagant.

The next morning, I asked Melissa what their story was. She explained that they weren't trust fund babies — it was their job to live on that boat as crew for the owner. For the majority of the year, it was just them living on the boat, having the time of their lives. Then, for the few weeks of the year when the boat›s owner came down for vacation, they uniformed up as the boat›s professional crew. I was floored. I didn't know a job like this even existed.

In the days that followed, I got to experience Melissa and Scott's simple and beautiful daily life. Each day was different. Some days we went surfing, spearfishing, or on lobster-catching missions. Every day there was work and care to be done for Kaimana, making meals, cleaning, and boat repairs. Some days, depending on the weather, the surf, and how everyone felt, we would sail to a different island. There was no microwave or television on board, and it seemed to be an unspoken rule that all activities must be paused to appreciate the sunset each evening. Scott's version of watching high definition television was to flip on the under-ship lights at night and blast East Forest's song "10 Laws" at top volume while we gazed out at the water glowing neon blue. Nights were spent wrapped in blankets on the bow tripping out on the absolutely obscene night sky where shooting stars shot across every few minutes and the Milky Way seemed more like a low-lying cloud than an entire galaxy. Life was slow and centered around appreciating life and the natural world.

I marveled at Melissa and Scott, who had left everything to live this completely different kind of life. I told them how they were opening my eyes to new possibilities. Scott smiled with a mischievous twinkle in his eye and handed me a book called *The High Line*, written by his friend Dusty Middleton. I started reading, and found that it was, of course, a collection of short stories about ordinary people who had life awakenings. For most of the characters in the book, this meant that they left their traditional lives for lives on 'the high line,' quitting their traditional jobs to live on boats or islands or mountains, working low-pay, high-satisfaction jobs, and traveling. Whatever the individual iteration, I saw this high line as a place where your lifestyle and soul were aligned.

As I read the book and settled into the adventure and simplicity of boat life, my creativity and energy began to grow. The new experiences opened my eyes and lit me up like a child. I started writing like I couldn't keep the words inside of me. Each morning I woke early and climbed to the very top of Kaimana to watch the sun rise and write. I grinned like an idiot up there by myself, thinking over and over again, "I'm so happy to be *alive*."

Atop Kaimana one morning, the thought of my impending return to 'real life' crept up in the back of my mind. A knot formed in my gut. I didn't want this feeling to end. I started fantasizing about living on a boat myself, and my mind began to wander. I imagined what my life would be like if I didn't work at a nine to five job in a corporation anymore. I started musing and wrote a list of other jobs I could have:

Alternative Lifestyle Options

Boat crew [chef] — culinary school?
Live on a boat
Live on an island — freelance writing?
Teach English somewhere
Buy land; open a pension / B&B
Open TATER in Austin for income

I looked over my list with a feeling of longing. Then, a huge light bulb went off in my head (or my soul?). *I am in control of my life*, I thought. I don't have to work at a desk. I don't have to live in Austin. I don't have to live the life I think will make my parents happy. My life is mine to do with as I please. And there are so many wild and wonderful possible lives to lead!

For the first time in my 30 years alive, I was struck with the realization that I could do whatever I wanted with my life.

I sat back, watching the sun rise over Bora Bora. I saw with clarity how I had been blindly following the en masse blueprint of what I thought I was supposed to do. I felt my soul's pull to live a life that lit me up inside. I thought about my lifelong dream to travel and experience more of what the world had to offer. I envisioned leaving my job and starting a new chapter of life on the road, exploring the world. It felt so right, but I was filled with doubt: *Could I really do this? Would it be worth it? Why not just wait until retirement like I'm "supposed" to?*

Those questions led my thoughts to Stephen, Ivan, Mallory, and Dan.

Before Mallory was killed at 27, I would sometimes judge her for her choice to work as a bartender after she had graduated from college, unlike me, who put my degree toward a "real job" and was "successful." Now, I realized the joke was on me. Mallory had found something she loved doing and was good at. She had a tight network of friends who loved her. It was *I* who was unhappy.

It hit me: I was not living, only existing.

The lesson I learned when Dan died, that life isn't meant to be lived in fear of death, meshed then with my new realization that I possess full autonomy over my life. All my friends who had died unexpectedly at young ages were real life examples that death can come at any time; there is no time to waste.

The many fears I had about veering from the blueprint seemed, now, insignificant. I didn't care much what people would think of me, about how much money I made, or about venturing onto an unknown path. If I knew I was going to die tomorrow, there would be no question — I would start living my authentic expression of life now.

I made up my mind. I would travel the world for a year — a 'mid-career temporary retirement' of sorts. My version of living on the high line. A feeling of peace came over me, and I smiled, remembering Dan's 'adventure awaits.' I had found mine. My half-joking hopeful prediction had proven to be true: In Tahiti, I figured out my life.

* * *

During my remaining days on Kaimana, I thought through the logistics of how to make a year of traveling work: responsibilities, job, money, and so on. I was divorced, so no more husband to worry about. I had my dog, Pajamas, but I knew my parents would be more than willing to take care of her for a while. I had recently finished paying off my student and car loans and begun saving money from my paycheck each month. I would have to save significantly more, but I was prepared to do whatever it took to make that happen. Finally, despite the golden handcuffs and ego fluff I got from working my fancy corporate job, I felt ready to move on into the scary unknown.

I still plan on opening my potato-themed food truck someday. I mean, who doesn't like a simple and wonderful dollop of mashed potatoes or an order of perfectly crispy french fries with a cold beer on the side? But this — this dream — was first.

I returned to Austin bubbling with my fresh perspective and excitement for my plan. I started telling everyone I knew that I was going to quit my job to travel around the world for a year. Well, everyone except my boss, of course. With lots of research and some dumb luck, I calculated that to make this fly financially, at a bare minimum, I would need at least six more months at my job with hardcore saving and penny-pinching.

I had the stroke of dumb luck on the flight back from Tahiti. I happened to sit next to a jolly British man who was, wouldn't you know, traveling around the world for a year. He was on the final leg of his trip and plenty chatty, so I spent the entire flight interviewing him about logistics: how he budgeted, what he spent, what he had learned along the way. He told me that prior to the trip, he planned to spend US$50 per day, but that he should have budgeted US$80 per day.

That sounded reasonable to me until I got home and actually multiplied 80 dollars by 365 days. I definitely did *not* have thirty grand sitting around, and my calculations showed that it would take me more than a year to get anywhere even close to that. Even his original budget of $50 would be $18,250 for the year. I realized that if I wanted to make this dream happen now — and I felt a fiery urgency not to put it off — then I was going to have to figure out a way to travel for less.

I thought back to my conversation with the British man and remembered how he had spoken extensively about the souvenir shopping he did around the world: custom clothing in Thailand, art in Turkey, his plan to buy a pair of genuine cowboy boots once he touched down in the US. I resolved that on my trip, I would be incredibly selective about any material goods I might purchase.

I also considered the highest costs of travel: airfare and lodging. I remembered how I had gone to Italy using airline miles. I only had to pay for the taxes; it cost me $10.50! I started researching how to earn airline miles using credit cards. There are people who use extremely elaborate systems, but just by doing the basics — signing up for a card that offers bonus miles, which I did with four cards — I banked somewhere around 120,000 miles, essentially for free. Most of the travel hackers I followed online spent their miles on first-class seats. Don't get me wrong — I have had the privilege of flying first class twice in my life thanks to miles and a family pass, and it is divine. But to maximize my miles, I would only fly the cheapest class on the cheapest days. I researched more ways to make long-term travel work financially, and I incorporated the ones I liked into my trip plans: work trade for lodging, house sitting, slow travel, cooking my own meals, and remote freelance work.

I had returned home from Tahiti in June. Six months to save money meant I could depart in January. A month's notice would have me notifying my boss after Thanksgiving. My timeline was set.

After my shipmates in Tahiti, my parents were the first people I told. I sat them down at their kitchen table and told them I was going to do this thing that was meaningful to me before it was too late. To say they were shocked would be an understatement. And to say they were comfortable with me quitting my job and traveling around the world solo would be a flat-out lie. But they knew I'd made up my mind. They asked lots of questions about my reasons and the logistics, but they never once tried to talk me out of it. Ultimately, they were supportive, as they had been throughout my life. They also said they would, of course, take care of Pajamas.

Next, I told my then "boyfriend." I use quotes here because, as I mentioned earlier, although I was head over heels for him, between me being out of the dating game for a decade and him never having had a girlfriend, we had no idea how to do a relationship. For seven months we had been in the ambiguous state of *acting* like boyfriend and girlfriend, but we never actually talked about whether we were.

When I told him about my plan, I expected the reaction of a friend with benefits, but I got the reaction of a boyfriend. He froze at the news and said there was no way he could get away from work for any amount of time. This was followed by an awkward moment in which we both realized I had already known he couldn't come. Not knowing what to do, we proceeded in our "sort of" relationship without bringing it up again. Ah, avoidance.

Nevertheless, my excitement grew. I told some of my closest coworkers, friends, and family. I also told the cashier at Trader Joe's and the lady I didn't know outside of our chats at the dog park. I received reactions ranging from shock and discomfort to support and joy. I told lots and lots of people my plan because I had been conditioned by Google to share ideas widely. It's rooted in collaboration and progress; the more people you talk to about your idea, the more feedback you'll get, and the more real and evolved it becomes.

I had been in a book club for two years for which I had completed precisely zero of the books. I read parts, enough to keep up in the conversations, but despite not actually reading the books, I stuck with the club because the women were bright, open, and vulnerable with each other.

With them, I felt like I had found my tribe. We talked some about the books, but mostly about our deepest thoughts and feelings and what we were going through in life. At the first book club meeting after my trip to Tahiti, I didn't just tell them about my plans for the next year. I shared my entire experience of tragic losses, the intense death anxiety I had suffered as a result, and about how, ironically, it was another tragic death that caused me to radically alter my perspective on life and death.

"But why now?" Katrina asked when my story finished with the news about my decision to embark on what I was now calling my "Soul Vacation."

"Because you might die tomorrow," I replied matter-of-factly, surprising even myself. No one spoke, my words hanging in the air.

"That's it!" I cried, startling everyone at the table. "That's my book!"

They say that inspiration hits you like a bolt of lightning. That's how I felt when I realized I wanted everyone in the world to feel as vibrant as I had since I'd realized that death is life's greatest teacher, that the finite nature of life is what makes it so precious, and that the best way to live meaningfully is to follow your bliss.

I had loved reading and writing since I could grasp a book. It was my solace, my source of growth and, for the better part of my life, the only way I could process emotion and engage vulnerably. Being a writer was my second dream career, after rock star (I mean, let's be real here). I had always wanted to write a book but had never before felt gripped by an idea for one.

I knew this message of urgency, life, and death needed to be shared with the world. It felt like everything I had experienced in my adult life had led me to this idea. I had no idea what I was doing (and still don't), but I raced home from the book club and wrote the storyboard for this book on big poster paper. The words and concepts flooded out of me and onto the paper.

This was the beginning of You Might Die Tomorrow, but it was also the beginning of a new phase of my life. I found a way to positively impact the world.

CHAPTER 5:

LEAVE THE WEAK
IN YOUR WAKE

It must be said that I am admittedly a naïve optimist with nary a shred of cynicism in my being. I've identified a pattern in my life in which I assume every situation is going to work out, and then, if things go wrong, I am shocked and awed and my face melts like Edvard Munch's painting *The Scream*. The pattern repeats again and again with my same genuine and complete shock every time things go wrong, even though roughly zero situations have worked out exactly as I initially planned.

Later that day, after the book club and my flood of creativity, I went to meet my "boyfriend" at a coffee shop. We had never once in our relationship hung out in any coffee shop, anywhere, but no warning bells signaled on my end when he requested to meet me at 2:00 p.m. at Genuine Joe's.

With excitement up to the skies, I told him that I had come up with a concept for a book that I thought could change people's lives. He listened quietly and then said he had something to share, too.

"I don't think we should see each other anymore, Kate."

It hit me like ten thousand pounds of coffee beans. I was shocked sick; I had no idea this was coming. He went on to say that he didn't see the point in dating someone who was going to be leaving for a year. I sputtered tactless words about how I thought he could date someone else while I was gone to get more experience being in relationships. It was no use. He had no idea how much I loved him because I had never said it. And I had not realized, until then, how much it had affected him that I was going to leave him behind.

I wish I could say that I was so high on life and had such a clear perspective on what really mattered to me that I brushed past this speed bump with grace. Not so. I fell from the high skies where I had been soaring down, down, down into heartbreak. I had experienced the pain of my marriage ending, but this was the first time I had been blindsided by rejection. What followed was real, deep heartbreak. Have you felt it before? That feeling of grasping for answers. Of pummeling your own self-worth. Of not getting off the couch for at least a week. It *hurts*.

In my heartbroken state, I began to question everything: What the hell do I think I'm doing with this crazy dream? I've lost a person I loved over this, and I haven't even left yet. It's such a colossal expense and a risk on so many levels. Traveling the world by myself? For a year? Absurd, too hard, unknown, and terrifying.

In my dark nights of fear and self-doubt, two things saved me: my ego and a sailor. My ego kept me from backing out of my idea, and a message from Scott lifted me back to being stoked on life.

My ego. When consoling me about my breakup, my sister said, "Don't be sad. In a few months, you'll smile about all this on a beach in Australia." This was not the empathetic response I hoped for, but it was exactly what I needed in order to realize that I had made my bed, and now I was to lie in it. I had blabbed my idea to everyone who would listen and their dog, and now my ego shoehorned me into a place where I couldn't back out. I had told everyone about my plans before my fear crept up. Two people had already told me they'd booked trips inspired by me. That's powerful, and also embarrassing. I inspired someone and then chickened out myself? Not me, no how. I'm proud as hell, and too stubborn to let that happen.

The sailor. As a first in my life, after getting dumped and falling into despair, I actually reached out to my family and friends for help. The 'please sit on the phone with me while I question everything' kind of support was generously given to me, in particular by my supportive sister Kelly and my wise friend Katrina. I poured out everything. I even sent my sob story to Melissa and Scott via their GPS texting device. In return, I got a text message from Scott that zapped me back into full-zeal-for-life mode:

FROM Kate 26 Aug 2015 14:28: I got dumped. He broke up with me because he doesn't see a future with someone who will be traveling around the world for the foreseeable future. I'm heartbroken. :(

FROM Kaimana Melissa & Scott 26 Aug 2015 15:48: Leave the weak in your wake. -Scott

With that powerful and simple message, I put my big girl pants back on, now with even more resolve to do the epic shit I had planned to do. *I will share the message about living like you might die tomorrow. I will take this trip. I will change the world.*

The next morning, I woke up early to the sun shining through my window. I took Pajamas out, then returned to my bed with its white sheets. I pulled out my laptop and wrote this journal entry:

Good Morning

It's unusually cool out this morning; I can feel the air seeping through the cracks of my old windows as I lie in bed. Moments later, as I step through my front door with my spotted dog on the end of her leash, the cool air envelopes me. I smile, and I am happy to be alive.

I was back on fire. I bought the youmightdietomorrow.com domain name, created a website, and the above entry became my first post.

At Google, the founders tell employees to do things that are "uncomfortably exciting." The idea is that if you're at least a bit scared of your idea, it might be big enough to make a difference in the world. I'd say uncomfortably excited is a pretty good description of how I felt about my new life path.

And that's how it went: I would swing from thrilled to terrified. I had serious concerns about whether I was crazy for doing something so radical, and so did a lot of other people. My dad tried to convince me not to quit my job. People would ask me point-blank, "Are you sure you're brave enough to do this?" I struggled deeply with the idea of going into the unknown, of breaking from the pack. But I stayed resolved. To protect my ego, of course, and because I could not shake the feeling of *right* I had felt since the day I realized I could create my own life story, and that the unexpected nature of life and death meant I must start living for today. Full of doubts and fears, I pressed on, though I longed for a sign that I was on the right path.

A month later, I got it.

One day in September, I went into work to find my California-HQ bosses unexpectedly at the Austin office and a mandatory meeting for the whole team on my calendar. At our boss-free breakfast before the meeting, my team and I fearfully speculated about what was about to happen. Did we do something wrong? Are we getting a new boss? Are we changing departments again? We were clueless.

The time came for the meeting, and we silently filed into the room and took our seats at the big conference table. The bosses entered and began setting up the presentation screen. The tall, skinny one with curly hair folded his hands across his chest, and then broke the news:

"This team in Austin will no longer exist and is instead moving operations to New York City. You have three options: One, move to New York City and join the new team there. Two, on your own, find a new job at Google, in Austin or elsewhere. Three, leave the company with a severance package equal to three months' pay."

He paused to let the news sink in. I looked around in utter disbelief. Across the big table, one of my teammates began to quietly cry; the guy next to me put his head in his hands. Me — well, the gravity of the turn of events hit me. *I was going to get paid to leave the job I was already going to quit.* I felt like all the cosmos had aligned to deliver me an undeniable sign and a swift kick in the ass. I don't know that anything in my life had ever before fallen into place so flagrantly.

The boss went on to click through a presentation detailing more about the three options and our timeline to decide. I silently calculated my severance and vacation time payout and my existing savings. It was enough.

I knew that the layoff was a gift and sign to me, but in talking with most of my former teammates since, we have acknowledged that the job security rug being pulled out from under us was ultimately a gift to us all. Caitlin broke out of her comfort zone, taking the opportunity to parlay a new job at Google into yearlong international stints in Dublin and Sydney. Byron got a better job on a different team at Google. Brooke took the option to move to NYC, where she began dating her now-husband.

I, of course, took that severance package and ran far, far away — all the way to Australia. They had given us several months to make our decision, and in that time, I closed up my pretty little life in Austin, Texas to prepare for a year on the road.

In February 2016, I gave notice to my downtown Austin apartment, sold my car and many of my belongings, toasted goodbye to my Austin friends, and hugged my family and pup for the last time, at least for a while.

On one of my final days in town, I walked through my vacant apartment and thought about where I started when I rented it: newly divorced, suffering from low self-esteem and crippling death anxiety, hopeful but broken. The apartment was all white: floors, walls, ceiling — exactly how I felt when I rented it: a blank page ready for a new story. My story in the year and a half between move in and move out was exciting, unexpected, and pivotal. I fell in love again and later found myself with a broken heart, I hosted parties for dear friends, lost a role model on Everest, and discovered truths about life, death, and meaning which changed my life.

Since Dan's death, my death anxiety had diminished — but I was thinking about death more than ever. I used the possibility of dying tomorrow as motivation to live my best life today. The thought crossed my mind again as I stood in the blank apartment, *you could die tomorrow.* I ran my hand along the kitchen counter that was no longer mine, surveying my life and the weird and wonderful turns in it. I imagined myself at the end of life, looking back on an alternate scenario, in which I perhaps stayed in this lovely apartment rather than going on the trip. I knew I would regret not having taken the risk to live bigger and more authentically. I wanted more. I wanted to *be alive.*

CHAPTER 6:

THE EVERYDAY
MAGIC OF TREES

In the end, I totally regretted going on the trip.

Just kidding. I didn't want it to end. I wound up on the road for two years instead of one.

The trip was a wild, challenging, life-affirming experience. It was a spiritual quest which pushed me to my edges, put new wrinkles on my brain, and humbled me. It was also really, really fun. In short, it was the best thing I had ever done, up to that point.

I started in Australia. I had convinced my bosses to let me work from the Sydney office for the final couple months before the layoff. On the way to my Airbnb, I chatted with my taxi driver, telling him excitedly that this was my first experience driving on the left side of the road. He responded with as much excitement as a photographer being asked to do some free work "for your portfolio."

At my accommodation, I chose to overlook the fact that the room was definitely not the one that had been depicted in the photos. In any case, it still had a lovely view overlooking the flower-filled courtyard.

Out on the streets, I marveled at the good-looking Australians I walked among. They were tan, fit, and very well dressed. Their clothes all seemed to be made of airy fabrics that were perfectly tailored to show off tanned limbs yet remain tasteful and chic.

The first glimmer of discomfiture flashed in my chest. My fabrics weren't right, I was mid-winter pale, and the weeks of goodbye toasts and dinners in Austin had caught up to my thighs. I tried to wave off the feeling, but I felt like I had when I started sixth grade in a new school in Iowa: grossly out of place and wanting desperately to fit in.

I wrapped up my first day with a yin yoga class, mostly to keep myself awake until my self-imposed anti-jet lag bedtime of 9:00 p.m. More lithe Australians poured into the yoga studio around me, men and women alike. My head buzzed with exhaustion. I awoke partway through class, probably moments before having been lightly snoring among the Aussie yoga gods stretching and flexing. I headed home afterward and fell asleep immediately.

The next morning, I awoke and smiled, remembering I was in Australia. I then began to notice red marks all over my legs. A rash? Chicken pox? A memory of the constant buzzing the night before flashed in my mind. Mosquito bites. At least thirty, just on my legs. I marveled in horror at my reflection in the mirror. My entire body was covered in bites.

So began my new routine in Sydney. I walked the forty five-minute journey to work each day, through the bustling Central Business District, over the Pyrmont Bridge to Darling Harbour. The office had an incredible view of the sparkling harbor, which was dotted by sailboats and small yachts. My days were long and dominated by work. Since I was leading teams in Brazil, I worked on three time zones: 6:00 a.m. meetings with California, days at the Sydney office, and 11:00 p.m. meetings with Brazil. I spent more evenings than I care to admit eating packaged snack food for dinner and hoping my Airbnb hosts didn't think I was as much of a loser as I felt I was.

Two weeks in, I realized the first leg of my Soul Vacation world tour was not at all what I had envisioned it would be. I hadn't seen much of the city due to long days at work. The women at the office were more of the well-tanned, well-tailored, and toned Aussies I had become mildly annoyed to see. I realized that as a blonde, I didn't stand out at all in Australia, other than for perhaps being a slightly fatter, much paler blonde than the rest, with clothes that didn't fit in and what probably looked like a frightening, contagious skin disease. My only Australian friend so far was a stray cat who popped through my window to bask in the sunlight on my bed from time to time. I was lonely.

But when friends and family inquired about how my trip was going so far, I lied and told them I was using the time to recharge after a crazy busy last few weeks in Austin. I wasn't alone for a lack of friends, gosh, I was *choosing* to be alone.

The weird thing was, I started to believe that white lie, and that attitude shift changed everything. After those two lonely weeks, I did begin to recharge. I started taking group exercise classes and tried everything from HIIT training to aerial yoga. I realized that traveling alone meant I was going to have to get used to dining at a table for one out in the wild. So, I started practicing the art of owning my solo dinners right on the front patio of restaurants, like a badass. I set up a few coffee dates with my colleagues at work and joined a dating app and a travelers meetup group.

A few days later, I met my first friend on a group wine tour, a warm, funny Brazilian woman named Camila. Then, I went on my first Tinder date ever with a guy who, coincidentally, was also Brazilian. He was sweet, handsome, and when he picked me up for the date on his motorcycle, I finally felt it. As the wind whipped my hair and my arms circled his waist from behind, I finally felt like I thought I'd feel as a woman traveling the world: happy and free.

My first travel lesson? "Be patient with yourself. Nothing in nature blooms all year." I had been beating myself up for, essentially, not being Australian, and for not having had a social calendar immediately upon arrival in a country in which I knew literally no one. I learned that I needed to let go of my fantasy travel life and embrace whatever this trip would bring.

My next destination was Indonesia, my first visit to an Asian country. My first stop was a week at a yoga and meditation retreat in northern Bali. I arrived at the retreat during dinner and as I approached the table, heard the animated chatter…all in German. It turned out that everyone, including all guests, the owner, and instructors, were German, Austrian, or Swiss-German.

It would turn out to be a blessing. As we got to know each other, I shared my story and my book idea. I was overwhelmed with their support for the message. They said this was something people in their culture needed to hear because so many people there worked too hard, approached life with a very serious attitude, and lacked a spark for living. It was one of the first times I had firsthand confirmation that the message would appeal to more than just American people.

During my week at the retreat, I was also exposed to how differently death is handled in other cultures. One day, the retreat owner said we were welcome to join the funeral ceremony taking place in the village that day, which also happened to be my birthday. After a special birthday breakfast, Dominique and I donned our colorful Kamben sarongs to cover our legs and headed on foot to the cemetery just around the corner from our retreat. We came upon a medium-sized plot of land with a shaded platform in the center. People were scattered about, sitting around wherever they could find a spot. Every square inch of the platform was occupied. On one half, a dozen men sat shoulder to shoulder, each holding a mallet and playing traditional Balinese percussion music — a *Gamelan* orchestra. The other half of the platform was covered with flowers and fruits, ornate palm baskets, a whole dried pig, and an array of gold vessels from which thin smoke drifted up. I noticed a live chicken flapping its wings in a basket at the foot of the altar. Presiding behind the offerings sat what appeared to be a priest performing elaborate rites.

We took a seat on the ground under the hot Indonesian sun. The priest's rites continued for the next hour, during which time people milled about and chatted pleasantly with their neighbors. Then, everyone rose to their feet and began walking up the road toward the ocean's edge. At the front of the procession, a young woman walked with a large framed photo of the deceased man. Behind, many people sang, chanted, and carried tall colorful umbrellas. At the water's edge, they set up a small altar on the ground and people settled in for the continuation of the ceremony. Some looked somber or sad, some had broad smiles, some were huddled in a circle on the ground, chatting and laughing arm in arm.

As an American and a German, two cultures conditioned to

maintain a somber visage at a funeral, we were surprised at the 'come as you are' atmosphere of the event. All emotions that were being expressed felt so natural, nothing contrived or withheld. Whether an individual exhibited joy, sadness, or ambivalence, it was all *okay*.

We were particularly surprised when a jovial ice cream man approached us in the middle of the gathering and offered to sell us cold, sweet relief from the heat. Yes, an ice cream man at a funeral. How could we refuse?

After we got our sweet treats (also an unexpected delight: Neapolitan-flavored ice cream sandwiched in a sweet bread roll), we got to chatting with the purveyor of cold deliciousness. It turned out he was the brother-in-law of the guy who died. He shared that a few months ago, the man, who was in his forties, had died unexpectedly from a fast-progressing, unknown illness. Reading the confusion on our faces, he said it was not uncommon for the Balinese funeral to occur weeks or months following the death. After the person dies, the family washes and buries the body, and once they have saved enough money to pay for a traditional funeral, the body is exhumed and cremated for the ceremony.

"But why does it seem a little like…a party?" I asked.

He smiled. "Death is a part of life and the great cycle. My brother is now on to the next phase. Today, we celebrate him."

At that moment, we looked up to see the deceased man's children walk together into the sea. They were fully clothed, clutching flowers and an urn. When the water reached their waists, they stopped and released the flowers and ashes into the sea. A few feet away, other children played and splashed in the water.

Soon, everyone turned and walked back to the village. What struck me most was the energy of the event, described simply by our ice cream man: death as a part of life.

The final lesson I learned in Indonesia will stay with me forever. After the meditation retreat, I traveled to a remote island few people visit, besides surfers in pursuit of great waves and the occasional diver. This was exactly why I chose it: to have the solitude to work on my book with the opportunity to also potentially meet a good-looking surfer. I quickly learned upon arrival that bad waves that season meant I was one of only a handful of tourists on the entire island. So, no surfers.

One afternoon, as I walked on the beach alone, I was greeted by a very excited middle-aged couple. The language barrier prevented us from communicating verbally, but they eagerly offered me some of the peanuts they were carrying. I smiled and accepted, which seemed to please them both. The peanuts tasted unusually delicious. I would later learn peanuts are one of the few crops locals are able to grow well on the island. As I cracked and ate a few of the wonderfully crunchy nuts, the couple spoke to me in Indonesian. They motioned to the expansive ocean in front of us, offered me more and more peanuts, and then I saw the woman's eyes grow wide.

"Bagus!" she said, admiring the bracelet on my wrist. *Bagus* was one of the handful of Indonesian words I had learned so far. It meant 'beautiful.' I had just purchased the bracelet back in Bali, but it was clear she was enamored with the piece. So, I took it off, motioned that it was a gift to her, and placed it on her wrist. She clutched her new piece of jewelry to her chest and beamed at me.

Without another word, she gently grabbed my hand and

marched me up the beach toward what looked like a hut. Inside, the surprised family greeted me and invited me into their home with huge smiles and lots of excitement. They showed me around the single room house. Though it had bare concrete walls, a dirt floor, and a single lightbulb hanging from the ceiling, it felt like a cozy home. There were colorful blankets on the one bed, a small array of floral teacups on the kitchen table, and the energy was warm and welcoming. Soon, I was whisked to a chair in the kitchen area, where they placed their baby in my lap and a hot cup of sweet Indonesian coffee in my hand. I sat, surrounded by what seemed like three generations of the family. The kids took turns showing me their teddy bears, the ladies pulled out the beautiful, hand-loomed textiles they had made, we played around taking pictures, and managed to communicate through gestures and laughs.

Eventually, as it began to get dark, I bid my hosts goodbye and set off on the beach back to my accommodation. I marveled at the experience. Here I was, on a remote island knowing absolutely no one, and a family had taken me in and made me feel welcome and doted upon. I was floored by their hospitality.

I then thought about how I had given myself umpteen excuses for not extending invitations to my friends and family to come visit or stay with me at my old place in Austin. I didn't have a proper dinner table, so I wrote off having friends over for a nice meal. I worried that my traveling friends wouldn't like staying in my cramped, studio-like setup that offered little privacy. I worried I wouldn't be an adequate host or Austin tour guide.

I saw now how I had missed so many opportunities to make the people I cared about feel welcome and loved in my home. Who cares if I didn't have a dinner table? The Indonesian family had managed to make me feel like a queen in their one-room, dirt-floor home shared by the entire family. I had had a perfectly lovely studio apartment to myself in an awesome location in downtown Austin, and yet had felt as if what I had wasn't good enough.

My new Indonesian friends taught me that it doesn't matter what you have, it matters that you share it with joy and love. They also taught me that going to museums and sightseeing is cool, but the personal connections one makes in travel are the most meaningful and memorable. It's a metaphor for life, actually. That's what matters most in life: people, relationships, and love.

I had created a rough itinerary for my big trip before I departed, but after my lessons in Australia and Indonesia, I decided to let go and see where this experience would take me. I had the privilege of road tripping around New Zealand with my sister for three weeks (see: brain-eating amoeba false alarm). I visited Scott and Melissa on Kaimana in French Polynesia again — twice. In celebration of Dan's life and to finally live like the adventurer I had always admired, I traveled to Nepal with Camila, that first friend I had met in Australia. We made the weeklong trek up to Annapurna Base Camp, danced at the top for Dan, and then spent several weeks volunteer teaching in a village outside of Kathmandu that had been ravaged by the 2015 earthquake. I went to Burning Man for the first time, which was one of Dan's favorite places. There, I had my mind blown by the experience and discovered that it was one of my favorite places, too. Over the span of just under two years, I visited twelve countries in all.

I would have to write a whole other book to give justice to all the juicy stories of adventure, love, mishap, and discovery (and I will write it, I promise). What I want to share with you here is the true resolution to this part of my life and my biggest lesson about living like you might die tomorrow. It didn't happen on the trip; it's about life after I got back.

See, when you're traveling to enchanting new destinations, it's not hard to be high on life and carpe each diem. In a foreign country, everything is novel: the grocery store, a trip to the post office, a walk along the street. Plus, I was on a high just by actually doing this big, bucket list travel dream I felt so passionate about. It was easy to feel like I was living every day like I might die tomorrow.

When I returned to Austin, I had to orchestrate and readjust to 'regular' life: apartment, a new job, bills, traffic. With everything I had learned about life on my spiritual quest, I thought I would gracefully transition back to stationary life like some kind of enlightened guru. Instead, I was human. I all but stopped the nourishing meditation practice I had begun while traveling. I had moments of useless frustration in traffic. I got worried about insignificant problems and about my future.

What I have learned in the year and a half since I returned is that traffic and bills and self-doubt are part of life, but they are not all of life. Neither are big, sweeping actions like quitting a job or going on a meaningful trip. Since my initially rough adjustment period, I have recognized the opportunity for a lifelong challenge: to live like I might die tomorrow every day. To live with zeal and joy when I am unloading the dishwasher after dinner, scheduling a routine dentist appointment, or working on a challenging project.

The art of the year since my trip ended has been integrating being grateful to be alive, *wherever* I am alive.

This lesson became most real to me a few months after I got back from my trip, on a perfectly ordinary evening walking my dog. I walked Pajamas every day after work, a few miles around the neighborhood, roughly the same route every day, meandering past the same houses, school, market, yards. It was pleasant. Routine. Enjoyable.

One evening on our walk, however, I began to notice the trees. It began with one tree, a magnificent Texas live oak. My eyes traced the expansive root system, starting at the base of the tree. Its roots took up the entire corner of the block. Its thick trunk stretched straight up and out into a network of six or seven stout, gnarled branches that stretched up to the sky and out the ends of the earth. My neck craned up to take in the fairy tale canopy of branches and leaves overhead, where I saw — and heard — all of it swaying gently in the breeze. Full of awe, the tree's chorus fell upon my being.

I continued my walk and began to notice all the trees. My God, the trees! There must have been thirty different kinds just on the residential street I walked along. Imagine how many variations there are on Earth: different colors, textures, heights, shapes, fruit-bearing, deciduous, evergreen, tiny, gigantic. And isn't each one so beautiful in its own way?

Entire ecosystems of birds and bugs and critters can exist in and around a tree. We eat fruit and sap, heal with leaves and bark. Kids play, adults trim. A whole world exists within and around this plant, and they live for potentially *thousands* of years. Imagine the change that has occurred around a tree throughout its' life, while it remains solid, fixed, silently observing.

Finally, I thought about how these trees give us life. How

I, every day, breathe the oxygen they offer. I was in complete and utter awe of something I had seen millions of times throughout my life and not given a second thought. I thought about how it was often the ordinary moments of my life where I felt most alive: catching sight of a beautiful blue sky while waiting at a stoplight, hearing my mom's infectious belly laugh, the exhilaration of sharing a vulnerable feeling with someone, the pain of feeling overwhelmed or not knowing what to do next. I began to think about the beauty of everything in our existence: trees, animals, life, nature, people, consciousness. Coffee is delicious. Flowers are exquisite. Cake! Love. Life is so beautiful.

It's all complex and awesome...and I thought I had to travel around the world to feel alive. I had gone on this trip, and it was a Big Meaningful Thing that I will, at the end of my life, surely feel satisfied to have done. But I learned that it is the Small Meaningful Things which make up the greater satisfaction of my life, in time and in value.

When she learned she was being awarded the Nobel Peace Prize, Mother Teresa was asked, "What can we do to promote world peace?" She answered, "Go home and love your family."

This chapter of my life taught me that living like I might die tomorrow is certainly doing big things — everything from getting divorced, quitting a job, going on a bucket list trip, and writing this book — to experiencing everyday awe in trees, really enjoying the deliciousness of mashed potatoes, and figuring out how to stay awake to the privilege of existence in daily life. In a life in which I have no idea why I'm alive or what meaning it has, I choose to create meaning that feels good to me and actively follow that bliss. In travel, in trees, in potatoes, and clouds, I'm just so happy to be alive.

PART II:

LEARN FROM PEOPLE WHO HAVE BEEN THERE

□

CHAPTER 7:

INTRODUCTION TO PART II

Okay, book's over. Now go out and live every day like you might die tomorrow.

Nah, I'm not going to leave you hanging like that. My story is not enough, it's just one example of a personal transformation thanks to a changed outlook on death. To cultivate your own transformation, you need more examples, scientific studies, and your own personal reflection. The rest of the book will further explore how one can cultivate a vibrant, death-embracing, life-affirming, meaningful life. You can do this, and it can change your life.

Let's start with learning from people other than me who have done it.

You know how, when someone dies, people say, "Hug your family a little tighter?" How terminally ill patients have a sense of urgency to live? How my experiences with unexpected death precipitated my massive shift in life perspective? Or how Dickens depicts Scrooge as miserly and unhappy until he sees his unkempt, unloved future tombstone, and, confronted by his mortality and the reality of a lonely legacy, he changes into a generous, warm man?

Death changes people.

Perhaps you have already had an experience of loss or a brush with death that caused you to look at life with a new set of eyes. Post-traumatic growth, or PTG, is the clinical name for an experience of positive psychological change as a result of adversity. The concept of emerging from a trial in life stronger and more grateful is as old as humanity, but the term PTG was only coined in 1995 by Richard G. Tedeschi and Lawrence G. Calhoun.

The growth in PTG occurs not from the crisis itself, but through the experience of grappling with the crisis. According to Tedeschi and Calhoun, in mentally and emotionally processing the traumatic event and re-adjusting to life after it, up to 89% of trauma survivors report one or more of the following feelings: a greater appreciation for life, closer relationships with others, seeing new possibilities in life, feeling stronger, and new or strengthened spiritual beliefs.

Experiencing a traumatic event, especially relating to the death of ourselves or someone we love, is one of the most challenging experiences in life. But the beauty of post-traumatic growth is knowing that there may be a brighter future after a dark time. Spiritual leader Thich Nhat Hanh uses the lotus flower, which grows best in muddy conditions, as a metaphor for transformation and growth through suffering. He says, "No mud, no lotus."

The lessons we learn from confronting trauma are typically not magical, overnight experiences of growth. They are muddy, tearful experiences of acquiring personal truth by having little choice but to face the realities of life and death. But from slogging through the muck, we can learn white lotus truths.

Loss and near-death experiences are not prerequisites for a radically new perspective on life, but they *are* effective catalysts.

Whether you have experienced death firsthand in your life or not, however, your ability to look at life as a precious gift is only a shift in perspective away.

But it's not easy to maintain clear perspective and awe for our existence day in and day out, especially without a wake-up call. This is where we have much to benefit from hearing the stories of people who have emerged from a confrontation with death with a new perspective on life. The lessons we can learn from those who have been there serve as a manual for the living on how to live and die well.

□

CHAPTER 8:

TRANSFORMATION AFTER LOSS: LEONARDO'S STORY

I met Leonardo at a place in northern California where the lush, otherworldly Redwood Forest meets the misty Pacific Ocean. It was at the most beautiful rest stop I have ever encountered, where the parking spots face a grove of imposing Redwood grandfathers who look down upon the cars. It feels as if you have pulled off into a fairy tale.

By 10:00 p.m. the night before I met Leonardo, all parking spots were filled with RVs and cars containing travelers and nomads like myself who were taking advantage of California's eight-hour rest stop parking limit. Before I tucked in to sleep in the backseat, I curled up with Pajamas, a glass of red, and a couple of chapters from *The Tibetan Book of Living and Dying*. I later dozed off to the sounds of waves crashing.

The next morning, I returned from brushing my teeth in the rest stop bathroom and noticed a bushy-haired young man standing behind my car, gazing at the You Might Die Tomorrow / So Live Today sticker on my rear window. He wore a ripped t-shirt and had a black bandana taming the curly mess on his head. He was lost in thought and I startled him as I walked up.

"That's a great sticker, man," he said, not breaking his gaze on the sticker. By this point, I was used to receiving comments on my sticker. Most gave way to the commenter acknowledging the truth in the sentiment and sharing a heartfelt personal story about how they came to believe it in life. Other comments were various iterations of, "That's so morbid," or "You could die today!" Regardless of the sentiment, I took every opportunity to prod the commenting individual for their deeper thoughts. Considering I was on a road trip with nowhere to be that day, I had plenty of time to do so with this guy.

"Oh, yeah? Why do you say that?" I asked.

"Because that sticker states everything I know about life. That's it." I nodded without saying anything, hoping he would continue. He did.

"I've been on my flow for two years now, thinking about everything. Why we're here, why stuff happens…"

"Your flow?"

"Yeah, driving, traveling around the country, thinking, trying to find the best place to rebuild my life. The two things I figured out are one, after everywhere I've been, this place is the best place, the magic land. And two, the only thing we know in life is that we could die at any moment, and the only purpose I can find for death is to teach the living what really matters."

I smiled at him. His words, spoken in a thick New York accent, were unexpectedly profound. I felt an immediate connection to this heavy metal-looking stranger.

"That's exactly it. Would you like to have a sticker?" I asked.

"Really? Yeah," he said, nodding incredulously.

"Absolutely. What's your name, friend?"

"I'm Leonardo."

We shook hands, and then I opened the back of my car, pulled out a fresh sticker and handed it to him. He immediately started playing with it, rolling the edges, fanning himself with it. He had more to say.

I prodded. "So, how did you come to this big realization about life and death?"

He continued to roll and unroll the bumper sticker loosely in his hand, now looking off into the distance.

"In the span of two years," he began, "everyone and everything I loved in my life died."

He broke his distant gaze to look me in the eyes before continuing.

"First, my dad died of a heart attack, out of nowhere. A year later, I held my mother in my arms as she took her last breath. Lung cancer. See, I'm from Little Italy in New York. Mulberry. I'm an only child. My parents were my everything. I came home every night, and they were there. Then I was alone."

"The next fucking year, my best friend committed suicide, and then my cat died. It was just...it was all over. My life had been completely blown up. Everything, and I mean *everything*, had been taken away. I had so many questions. Why did this happen? What did I do to deserve this? How can I go on? What the fuck am I supposed to learn here?" He took a breath.

"I had built up this successful tattoo business. I took a lot of pride in it, that I could do good work and give some of give my friends jobs who needed them. But after everyone and everything I cared about in life died, I gave it all up. I signed over the business to my friend. I just gave it to him. I packed up my car and started driving. I had no idea where I was going to go; I just needed to think. That was two years ago."

I could see the pain in his eyes, feel it radiating from his being. Pain, and confusion, and exhaustion from wrestling with the meaning of life and death.

He continued.

"The other thing I've figured out...," he trailed off for a moment.

"So, yeah, little Italy. Like, there's things you gotta do to be a real Italian. You gotta have the right Cadillac. The jewelry. And other stuff, you gotta watch your back when you're takin' out the trash; you could get your throat slit just taking out the trash. You get wrapped up in this stuff: what your friends think, the gangs, the material stuff. After all that stuff happened to my family and to my best friend, I realized I didn't want any of that. I don't care about the Cadillac. I don't want to worry about taking out the goddamn trash. But it took my whole family dying for me to figure that out. I now see that figuring the important shit from the bullshit is part of our purpose in life. I had to lose my entire family — everything I loved, my whole world — to figure out that, besides my family, what I thought was important wasn't what's important to me at all. I can't believe it took all that, but it did. And the funniest thing? The irony is absolutely killer. The stuff that we're taught to think is the most important in life, or even the stuff you think is important — ego shit — is the stuff that's that matters the least."

He paused his fidgeting with the sticker, now tightly rolled in his fist, and looked me in the eye.

"Nothing, nothing in life is guaranteed. My whole family died. What I know now is that I could go at any moment."

Almost breathless, he paused once more. The weight of the lessons learned hung in the air, lessons learned in agonizing grief by a man forever changed.

And then softer, with a shrug, he continued, "So, I choose to be out here, on my flow. I listen to NPR, I read books. I never did that before. I don't drink or smoke cigs, just smoke some weed. I found this amazing beach here, Moonstone Beach. I talk to my friends and relatives in the old neighborhood when I can, but I don't listen to them when they tell me to come back. I just want to be here for now, in this magic place where people let you be you, living a simple life and appreciating being alive. But…," he trailed off.

"There is one thing I need that I can't find."

"What is it?" I asked.

"Fucking good Italian food! Where I'm from in New York, every corner in Little Italy has the best food you can imagine. But we're picky, because we have so much to choose from. Everyone's got their place. Out here, man…naw." He laughed.

"I went to this place, Gino's Real Italian. This is one of a million terrible Italian food stories I can tell you, but I went to Gino's Real Italian. I love this place, northern Cali, but the food is just terrible. So I found this place, and I had high hopes, real Italian, right? It was awful. The tomato sauce, you have no idea. It was all wrong. They said it's pizza; it ain't pizza. Little Italy, I could go anywhere. The worst place there is a hundred times better than the best place out here. They don't know how to do it. Out here, it's more about the quality of ingredients. Organic this and that, it's good stuff, but they don't know how to put it *together*. They think it's good, but it's not good. The pizza here will have twelve toppings on it, artichoke and spinach and all the stuff, but they can't even get the sauce right!"

He smiled. "So, I'm really okay now, but the only thing I don't have is good food. I live on the road in this gorgeous place with amazing, peaceful people but the only thing I don't have is good food."

We continued to stand there for two hours, a couple of strangers, talking about anything and everything. We talked about life, death, space, conspiracy theories, and what makes us happy. He told me about his drive from New York, zig-zagging across the country. He gave me directions to that special Moonstone Beach, and then we parted ways.

I never saw Leonardo again, but his stories and lessons will stay with me forever. What struck me about Leonardo was the peace I sensed in him. He had experienced tragic loss, but I could see that day that Leonardo emerged with a new outlook on what's important in life and an ability to appreciate the simple joys of being alive. I do hope he finds his real Italian meal, though.

◻

CHAPTER 9:

THE SURVIVOR'S
PERSPECTIVE

Remember that time I thought I had a brain-eating amoeba? While that *felt* like a near-death experience to me, it was purely hypochondria. Since ancient history, thousands of accounts have been recorded of people who have come close to true biological death or have even clinically died but survived. It's what is commonly referred to as "seeing the white light" in an out-of-body experience when in a physically grave state as a result of illness or injury. Surveys by the International Association for Near-Death Studies suggest that 4-15% of the population have had near-death experiences, or NDEs. Their prevalence and fascinating nature have led to physiological, psychological, and transcendental factors associated with the NDE by psychologists, neuroscientists, researchers, spiritual groups, and enthusiasts all over the world.

There is not a widely agreed upon explanation for NDEs. Science-based explanations include a limbic system response, the effects of anesthesia, and hallucinations as a result of a lack of oxygen to the brain, to name just a few. The most common nonscientific explanation is of divine intervention, that God or a greater power sent the person "back" to life.

Many of the people who have had a near-death experience also report a significant shift in their outlook on life as a result. In Anita Moorjani's bestselling book, *Dying to Be Me*, she shares her gripping and moving account of her near-death experience and its profound effects on her life. When I listened to the audiobook during nightly walks with Pajamas, I would race out the door with excitement each evening to hear more of the unbelievable story.

Anita's body had been ravaged by aggressive lymphoma. One day, shortly after she was told she wouldn't make it through the night, she entered a coma. The next day, to the shock of her doctors, she awoke. Still very much alive, she recounted a vivid near-death experience in which she perceived the whole of mankind and existence as a dazzling tapestry all woven together, with her and the whole of her life's experiences as a single thread woven into the infinite creation. Remarkably, Anita's body was cancer-free just four weeks after her miraculous awakening from the coma. Her ultimate takeaway? Live life with joy and abandon. Having experienced what it's like to die, Anita returned to life with, in her words, "the freedom to be me." She felt freed from the chains of living life for anyone or anything else but her own bliss and for love.

Dr. Kenneth Ring is a respected psychologist and researcher who has meticulously researched NDEs since the late 1970s. As a psychologist, he concerned himself not with proving or disproving NDEs, but with cataloging the common experiential elements of a transcendental near-death experience and the often life-changing aftereffects.

First, his research shows that subjects mainly report that dying isn't scary. On the contrary, Dr. Ring found in his research that NDErs report the experience of dying to be one full of positive emotions: peace, comfort, unconditional love and acceptance, often including a life review and insight into the nature of the universe. That sounds pretty ideal to me.

Second, he reports that death can imbue marked clarity about one's priorities in life. Among people who have experienced a transcendental NDE, Dr. Ring identified a consistent set of value and belief changes. In his words:

"They're profoundly appreciative of being alive. They've got a greater sense of self-worth and care more deeply for others and are able to give love more freely. Another thing that happens to them is they become less materialistic and less concerned with success in conventional terms. They lose their ambition to achieve by ordinary criteria for a successful life. Instead they may be very interested in helping others. They may change their occupation. For example, an accountant might become a nurse."

This is not a cause and effect situation, however. Just as many traumatic experiences don't result in post-traumatic growth, not every brush with death results in the psychological near-death experience — and not every NDE results in a positive aftereffect.

Dr. Ring estimates that only one in three people who come close to death will have a "transcendental" near-death experience, meaning that two out of every three people who almost die just... almost die. No white light or life review or positive feelings. Just like a trip to the figurative grocery store and back. For that majority, the feeling after almost dying is less, "I've been profoundly enlightened!" and more "Holy shit, that was close."

At some point, we've all had that acute realization that had things gone a little bit differently, we'd be dead. Allergic reactions, car crashes, stepping out into the street at the wrong moment,

misdiagnoses, contemplation of suicide, natural disasters —
we're in potentially deadly situations every day (I mean, let's be
honest: I'm a terrible driver). But if every brush with death were a
life-changing, enlightening experience, we'd all be walking around
as Buddha and you wouldn't be reading this book.

Similarly, we know people, perhaps including ourselves, who
experience the death of someone we love and vow to live life
differently, only to go right back to our old ways.

So, if almost dying or experiencing the death of someone close
to us isn't a guarantee of having an awakening, how the heck do
we get those benefits?

Perspective.

That's really all the positive aftereffects of near-death experience are, a shift in perspective. An NDE is an example of being
exposed to an experience that changes one's outlook. Like reading
this book could do, or imagining you have a brain-eating amoeba,
or talking to someone who has a terminal illness...or thinking
about how wild it is that you just survived a drive down a highway
at speeds in excess of sixty-five miles per hour in a metal box on
tiny wheels. To cultivate the near-death mindset, you need not put
yourself in danger. You already are.

The reality is that we come close to dying every day. Each
time we make it to our destination safely, recover from the flu,
return home after a jog, or hoist ourselves out of the pool after a
swim, we have evaded death. Life is a terminal condition. If you
open yourself up to the near-death experience of being alive, you
— like those who have actually been on the verge of imminent
biological death — may cultivate a more grateful, compassionate,
joyful life perspective.

CHAPTER 10:

WHAT NOT TO DO

In 2009, Australian palliative care nurse Bronnie Ware wrote a blog post called *The Top Five Regrets of the Dying* that shot to popularity, read by more than three million people in its first year. For years, Ware sat by the bedsides of dying people, held their hands, met their families, bathed them, and, most importantly, listened to them. In the article, she reported to the world the five salient regrets expressed by the great majority of her patients facing imminent death.

Following are each of the five most common dying regrets cited by Ware's patients with anecdotes and reflections on each. For the living, they are a guide for how *not* to live. I encourage you to think about each of these regrets and consider whether you might have this regret if you continue to live your life as you are now. Then, think about how you can change your actions and thoughts to live in a way that will lead to you feeling fulfilled instead of regretful at the end of your life. The people on their deathbeds who expressed these regrets had little time to live differently. But those of us not on our deathbeds have the gift of the possibility of time to right the ship.

#1. I wish I'd had the courage to live a life true to myself, not the life others expected of me.

If this regret resonates with you, you are likely living one of two ways: for the perceived ideals of others, or on autopilot, just doing what you think you should do without thinking much about what *you* want to do.

For whom are you living? Are you checking your gut when you make decisions, or are you living for the perceived expectations of your parents, societal ideals, or the Joneses? Maybe you largely base your life choices on how you think you will look to others. Here's the irony: living for others' ideals to gain recognition or love makes you blend in. It's incredibly difficult to stand out by doing what everyone else is doing; you basically have to be the best. There are very few bests, and you'll likely regret having wasted your life.

Make sure you are checking your own gut, living vibrantly, and being your weird and wonderful self. You may be surprised that this wins the attention and accolades you seek. And rest assured, some people will proverbially mall walk away, eyes bulging, and eyebrows raised. Let them walk. You'll get to die knowing you lived as the real you.

You might be on autopilot if you are blindly checking off the boxes of the "expectations" of modern society. Philosopher Martin Heidegger argues that humans have two modes of being. The first is the 'everyday' mode in which we allow ourselves to be pulled in various directions toward daily obligations, are mired in stress, and allow time to pass without feeling the moment. In this mode, you're living a life others expect of you, but you're doing it less to actively please others and more because you're just following the "blueprint," not thinking about why you're doing much of anything.

The second is the 'ontological' mode. This is the good stuff, people. It's the mindful, authentic mode in which we feel the moment, have a more 'zoomed out' perspective, and think about that which is truly important to us. This is the mode in which you stop for a moment to look up at the sky, smile, and remember that you are *alive*.

If you are largely stuck in Heidegger's "everyday" mode and going along like that dandelion seed or building your life around an ideal other than your own, you will die regretful of having wasted your only opportunity to be the fully expressed iteration of you.

It may not be practical to trip out on the magnificence of every tree you see, but what about taking a moment each morning when you wake up to appreciate being alive? To shift your balance to favor that peaceful, authentic ontological mode would minimize the potential regret of having wasted your life by living for someone else's expectations and improve your quality of life. How, then? Some ideas: slow down, appreciate nature, seek awe, meditate, prioritize enjoying your life, contemplate your mortality.

"And every day, the world will drag you by the hand, yelling, "'This is important! And this is important! And this is important! You need to worry about this! And this! And this!'" And each day, it's up to you to yank your hand back, put it on your heart and say, "'No. This is what's important.'"

-Iain Thomas

#2. I wish I hadn't worked so hard.

In practice, this regret is a derivative of the first regret Nurse Ware identified, living for others' expectations instead of our own desires.

Let's not mistakenly demonize work. Work is a source of survival, it can make a worker feel alive, and, for some people, it *is* a profound source of meaning and purpose — and I'm not just talking about humanitarian workers. Did you hear the one about the Mayo Clinic janitor? He was asked by a documentary film crew doing a piece on-site whether he was cleaning up for the next patient. The janitor replied, "No. I'm saving people's lives." He explained that unsanitary conditions and bacteria are a real threat to life in health care facilities and that he felt a sense of duty and purpose by saving patients from those dangers by doing his work well.

What matters is the meaning and purpose we get from our work and our balance of time spent working and time spent on other life priorities and pursuits. The dying regret of working "too hard" is probably a misuse of the word "hard." If you derive meaning and purpose from your work, you won't likely regret spending your Life Time on it or giving 100% of your energy at work. However, if the *time* or *energy* you put into work is inflated relative to your other life priorities, like family, fitness, or one's true joy of collecting rare marbles, there will be regret at having misspent your precious time resource.

I think people actually mean they regret working *too much*. The regret of working too "hard," then, is rooted in an imbalance of how an individual expends their Life Time on work versus other meaningful life priorities. Stick around to the end of the book for the Delta Assessment which will make crystal clear to you whether your meaningful priorities in life are aligned with how you're actually spending your time.

And now, a special shout out to all of you folks who are working a job that isn't saving any babies but does pay the bills. There's nothing wrong with you or your job. That is, unless you are spending too much time on it or are actively unhappy in it. Then, without an urgent change, you may be setting yourself up to be saddled with the regret of having wasted your life at work.

Working too much? Whatever the pull is that has you over-performing or overspending your time — a demanding boss, a desire for material goods that don't bring you inner joy, a desire to be respected, or even a sense of boredom in other aspects of life — know this: you are in control of what you put into your endeavors. You have power and choices in your life. You are in control of how you allot your precious Life Time.

Not finding enjoyment or meaning in your job? Hate going to work every day? You have three options:

1. Quit. Change to a role or job that excites and challenges you.
2. Don't quit; change nothing. Remain unhappy and unfulfilled.
3. Don't quit. But change your perspective. Find a Mayo Clinic janitor-like "why" for your work. Re-balance the time you spend on it accordingly.

The first option is ideal but not always possible. But if you have the spark and opportunity (and let's be honest, opportunity is largely just the way we look at things), I urge you to act immediately, before that spark dies out. You might feel burdened by your monthly budget or debt, but you still have options. Sell your stuff, downsize your lifestyle significantly, then allocate those proceeds and savings to pay down your debt. Easier said than done, to be sure, but entirely possible with a shift in perspective and a drive to make meaningful change.

If the first option is enticing to you, at a minimum, get out there and map out some ideas. What could you do to make money that you would also enjoy doing? If your dream job has a lower income potential, then how can you simplify your life and reduce your expenses? What do you spend money on that doesn't bring you happiness? What does your ideal life look like when you strip away societal ideals and just think about what fulfills you?

The second option sucks and may make you feel as if you've died. Zero out of five stars, do not recommend. Most of us have been there at some point, but let's not redo that and set ourselves up to be the dying person wishing they hadn't worked so wrongly.

Now, let's look at the third option. You've mindfully made the decision that you don't want to quit your job right now, but you're willing to do the work to change your situation there. Change your perspective, and your experience will change. Sound too good to be true? Unless there is verbal or other abuse going on, it's not. Here's an example.

I once had a boss who drove me crazy. He would look over my shoulder while I was working to check my work. He required team meetings every Monday morning, in which the first hour was exclusively dedicated to everybody sharing what they did over the weekend. In the afternoons, he would come out to where we were working and play loud 80s music. He was a huge personality that loved attention. I loved my job and the company, but I was at my wits' end.

The reality of the circumstances finally dawned on me: I wasn't going to quit, and he wasn't going to change, so the change would have to be in me. I decided to look at the situation objectively and was able to see something new. This guy wasn't intentionally doing these things to drive me, or anyone else, crazy. He was a guy with a heart of gold that wanted to help and be liked. He looked over my shoulder because he was curious about what I was up to, and, as a first-time manager, hadn't yet learned his boundaries or how not to micromanage. He asked us about our weekends because he wanted to foster camaraderie and so he could tell us about his own weekend motorcycle adventures. He interrupted our workdays with a jam session to show us that he was a cool, approachable manager and to foster a fun team atmosphere.

I decided to think of him as my real-life version of Michael Scott, the boss from the television show *The Office*, and my life at work as a hilarious, over-the-top TV sitcom.

This change in perspective lifted the weight off my shoulders and I started to enjoy my job much more. Where I used to feel frustrated and annoyed with his zany antics, I started to see humor and enjoyment in them. I would just laugh and shake my head. With my judgement and reactivity out of the picture, he and I forged a positive relationship. I could now see that he was a good person and a positive influence on those around him.

This person was Stephen, my manager at Google, whom you read about in Part I. A couple of months after I changed my perspective, I received the call that my 'Michael Scott' manager had died unexpectedly. I had no idea that it would be a life and death situation — but we rarely do. By stepping back and changing my perspective, I was able to relieve my stress at work and also see the good in my boss before he died.

The vast majority of us must work throughout our lives, in some capacity, to feed and shelter ourselves and our families, to be able to support causes we care about, to pay for travel, experiences, and passions, and to treat ourselves and the people we love. If you avoid allocating too much time to work relative to your other priorities and find some way to derive enjoyment from your experience working, you will set yourself up to feel good about this part of your life when you look back on it.

#3. I wish I'd had the courage to express my feelings.

In relationships, I've never been very good at sharing my feelings. I am excellent, however, at compartmentalizing them inside forever! I have often found myself with my feelings trapped in my heart, locked up tightly, sometimes inaccessible even to myself. I've realized I don't want to become a skeleton with my heart still battened down in steel plates and chains.

What I want is best expressed in the beautiful words of poet Sierra DeMulder:

"One day, you will learn how to give
and receive love like an open window
and it will feel like summer every day."

That day, however, can be today. To avoid dying with a heart locked up and a deathbed regret, we must open up. When your bravery flags, give the song "Smoke Alarm" by Carsie Blanton a listen:

> *He said baby what's the big deal*
> *Feel what you wanna feel*
> *Say what you're gonna say*
> *You're gonna die one day.*
> *...*
> *Why do you waste your time*
> *Thinkin 'bout your reputation*
> *Trying to meet an expectation*
> *Wonderin' what they're gonna say?*
> *When everyone you've ever known*
> *Is headed for a headstone.*

Opening up to another person is one of the most challenging things we ego-driven, anxiety-riddled humans can do. It can be terrifying. It is, therefore, among the best growth experiences. We pine for closeness, intimacy, and open love but allow our fear of vulnerability to supersede those needs. If we don't find the courage to open up, however, we end up on our deathbed with regrets about living our one life behind a mask.

Don't die holding on to anger toward your dad, without connecting deeply with your partner, or without openly expressing your love to your kids. Draw upon the potential of dying with this regret to summon the bravery and drive to open up and give and receive love like an open window every day.

Start small. Send a text message with a simple, "Hey. I love you." Write heartfelt birthday, Christmas, and just-because cards. It's often easier to express feelings in writing. Get the "scary" love stuff out of the way first; let "I miss you" or "I love you" be first thing you say when you see someone or answer their phone call.

Vulnerability begets vulnerability, and you might be surprised to find that your love and openness creates a safe space for others to do the same. Connect with people. It is, after all, only our love that will survive us.

#4. I wish I had stayed in touch with my friends.

Imagine you are viewing your own funeral from above. Who is there? How many butts are in those seats? Is anyone crying? Do all the people look like you? How many of them have you helped? How many of them really know that you loved them?

In the hundreds of hours of research I have done on life, death, and meaning, I have observed that in the end, the vast majority of humans find that all that matters are other humans. Relationships. Love. Bronnie Ware herself says, "Everyone misses their friends when they are dying."

Maintaining relationships is a lifelong process. If you want genuine connections in life and butts in seats at your funeral, you must reach out to people and do the work to sustain relationships while you're alive. Invite friends over for a home-cooked dinner, remember birthdays, and ask your loved ones questions about their lives and really listen to their answers.

Be patient and compassionate with yourself when you mess up. You will forget a birthday and sometimes get caught up in the hamster wheel of life and forget to reach out, like I did. Here is a story about my friend Caroline, who showed me how to valiantly save a friendship, even when things felt weird.

Caroline and I met in college and became inseparable. We were each other's source of support and understanding. Quick-witted and with a ready laugh, Caroline is the kind of friend who tells it to you *exactly* how it is but who will also sit and listen to you cry when you need it. After college, we moved to separate cities but kept in touch via long phone calls, emails, and the occasional cross-country visit.

Over the years, however, our lives diverged. I got divorced; she got married. I started my life traveling; she set up house and fulfilled her dream of being a mom. Somewhere along the way, a space crept up between us. We stopped calling each other, stopped emailing, and there were no more visits. Before we knew it, a couple of years had passed without a word other than a comment here or there on Facebook.

I missed hearing her laugh and I was dying to know what her life as a mom was like. I wanted her blunt, good-humored perspective on life. I missed my Caroline dearly but was wary because of the space between us. I wondered if she didn't want to be my friend anymore, if she was just too busy as a mom, or if she might be angry with me for some reason. I allowed these fears to supersede my desire to reach out to my friend. Then one day, she sent me this message:

"Hey Birthday Girl! I know it's not for a few days but it made me start thinking about you. I feel like it's been so long since we've talked to or seen each other. I know you've been busy with your travels and

writing a book, and I've been busy popping out children (I seriously need to stop), but I miss you. I miss having you in my life. I know we're in totally different places right now, and have been for a while, but I haven't forgotten about you, my friend, and think of you often. You doing ok these days? How's life? I hope you're well."

It was so unexpected, so stunning, and so beautiful. I was overcome with emotion. My dear, courageous friend said, "*to hell with the space*" and bravely reached out to me. With this one simple act of heartfelt outreach, Caroline broke ground on rebuilding the bridge between us.

This, my friends, is the example we should follow. Don't wish you had called when you weren't dying. Call now. Send the message now (Caroline said it's totally okay to just copy hers, minus the popping out kids part if that doesn't apply to you). Share your love now. To hell with space!

#5. I wish that I had let myself be happier.

Of her experience with dying patients, Ware says:

"Deep within, they longed to laugh properly and have silliness in their life again. When you are on your deathbed, what others think of you is a long way from your mind. How wonderful to be able to let go and smile again, long before you are dying. Life is a choice. It is YOUR life. Choose consciously, choose wisely, choose honestly. Choose happiness."

As you consider what you want to accomplish while you are still alive, how you want to live, and what you would like your legacy to be, what "bucket list" items cross your mind? Skydiving? Traveling to a far away land? Writing a book? Starting a business? Awesome.

Do not forget, however, that it is the small, everyday joys that will make up the greater satisfaction of your life.

It can be frighteningly easy to slip into the doldrum seriousness of life, to think insignificant things are significant, to be crushed by the weight of the rushing world, or to expend your life energy in the pursuit of ticking off the "boxes" of life in the belief that happiness lives just on the other side.

Prioritize not only the big things that are meaningful to you but cultivate those small moments of pleasure. Get on the floor and roll around with your dog, or your kids, or both. Go out in nature and just allow yourself to *be,* even for just ten minutes. Nowhere to go, nothing to do, just enjoy the experience. Turn on your favorite song and dance your freaking heart out in your kitchen. Get excited about little things that make you happy: when your food arrives at a restaurant, when you notice a lovely sunset, when you happen to hit all green lights on your way to work. When you wake up in the morning.

Try to see something good in every situation, even if it's just that the worst-case scenario didn't happen. Pop the bubble you have created around you and interact with the people and nature you come across in your everyday life. Do the damn gratitude journal. Let yourself be joyful, optimistic, and silly. Excitement is a "muscle" you can train, and it makes life a lot more exhilarating.

Remember when I said that if you don't like your job, you have three simple options? The same logic applies to any aspect of your life: change an external circumstance, don't change anything and be unhappy, or change your attitude. Happiness is a choice. It's not a permanent state of being you obtain. It's a mood. As spiritual teacher Sadhguru says, "Live life not in the pursuit of happiness, but as an expression of joyfulness."

When it comes to regret, we have a choice: amass more or take action now to avoid it. The constructive value of regret lies in our examination of it. Dr. Irvin D. Yalom counsels his regretful patients with these questions: "How can you live now without building new regret? What do you have to change in your life?"

Living with regrets is like climbing a mountain with a heavy backpack. The backpack is full of all the things you want to do in life: to enjoy yourself, to have the experiences you desire, to be truly yourself, to share your love. When you arrange your life to align with your true priorities, you empty the contents of that backpack as you go up the mountain — a phone call here, a vacation there, time with your kids here, helping others there. Then, when you reach the top of the mountain at the end of your life, you get to stand up there and feel the cool air on your face. You get to savor the feeling of looking back down at the trail, knowing you walked it as vibrantly and urgently as you could, and feel righteous in your life.

The alternative is obvious: you huff up that mountain, carrying the heavy backpack of the life you want to live the whole way up. At the top, sweaty and exhausted and with that heavy load still on your back, you realize you can't go back down and unload that pack. It's too late, life's over, and up here at the end of the trail, the weight will stay on your back forever.

CHAPTER 11:

AVOID REGRET:
THE DEATHBED GUT CHECK

Humans, by nature, are imperfect beings. We are also highly critical, especially of ourselves. While it's *possible* to die with zero regrets, for the majority of us, there will be things we wish we had done differently.

The idea of dying without regrets is less an achievable goal and more a worthy pursuit. Every single day, we can live actively working toward the goal of emptying our backpack of potential regrets while making peace with the fact that there will probably be a few articles left in the bottom or side pocket.

The notion of an incompletely realized goal may be difficult to swallow, especially for those of us who are perfectionists, competitive, or highly results oriented. But if the goal is instead the *sustained action* of living meaningfully and in alignment with your values, you'll also successfully mitigate regrets at the end of life. To strive to die without regrets will be the most incredible and gratifying quest of your life.

Performance visualization is a well-known technique used by elite athletes and performers to achieve success. Before a competition or performance, they mentally visualize themselves perfectly executing the play on the field, winning the race, or performing the piece on stage flawlessly. I apply this same concept to achieve fulfillment in life. I call it the Deathbed Gut Check and I use it regularly when I'm weighing how I should respond to a particular situation or to help me make tough decisions. It only takes five seconds.

The Deathbed Gut Check is the practice of visualizing yourself on your deathbed and, from that perspective, imagining how you would feel having made a particular decision in your life. On one's deathbed, all is stripped away. The petty and insignificant factors dissolve, and what's left is what's true and meaningful. Life's decisions are considered and given an honest grade. When faced with death, life is reduced to its simple, sweet syrup.

I start by picturing myself on my deathbed. It's admittedly an ideal deathbed. In a lovely beach house, I lie on white sheets in an airy, light-filled room filled with lots of fresh flowers (it's my daydream, okay?). I am surrounded by people I love. I know I will soon die peacefully and without fear, and that now is my chance to look back over my life and my decisions.

From this perspective, I consider the current decision I am weighing.

I imagine having chosen Option A and allow myself to feel how my body reacts to looking back on that choice. I pay specific attention to how I feel in my gut. Do I feel a lightness, content with Option A, or do I feel a heaviness at having chosen the wrong path? If it's not immediately clear, I repeat the visualization, looking "back" on my life, having chosen Option B.

The visceral feelings I feel may be subtle or quite strong, but they tell me everything I need to know. A sensation of regret might feel like a knot or a sick feeling in the pit of my stomach or a general uneasiness in my being. Maybe I feel guilt as a result of how my actions might have hurt someone else or disappointment that I made a choice to satisfy someone else's expectations.

When I consider the alternative option, I might feel a sense of surety, confidence, or merely a lightness of being. Sometimes, when I visualize making what I feel is the 'right' decision, a small smile creeps onto my face. I latch onto that feeling and honor it.

I've never found a better way to make everyday decisions and figure out what's important to me.

I want to live my life in alignment with my soul, meaning I want to make decisions that reflect my core values. When I act out of alignment with my soul, everything is off-kilter and feels out of control. I feel like I am slogging through muck, going through the motions of something that feels wrong, is wrong. I experience a sinking feeling, knowing that I'll regret what I'm doing.

The Deathbed Gut Check helps me avoid that feeling at all costs. It helps me tap into my own intuition, the purest sense of 'me,' unaltered by fear or external opinion.

The Deathbed Gut Check has helped me make life decisions great and small. Some examples of Deathbed Gut Checks I have done in the past:

Should I leave this job and chart off into this wild travel adventure? Four years ago, my Deathbed Gut Check said, despite the ego boost and nice amount of pocket change I'm getting from this job now, I'm not going to give a shit about having worked at a fancy tech company or having made a lot of money when I'm on my deathbed. I'm going to care about my depth of experience and, in the words of Mark Twain, will be more disappointed by the things I didn't do than the ones I did.

Should I buy this beautiful but expensive pair of shoes? My Deathbed Gut Check says no, I will not remember or care about these shoes at the end of my life, and that my money is better spent on an experience I will find meaningful when I look back on my life.

Should I hold onto my anger about what my partner did last week? Usually, my Deathbed Gut Check here says, no, I will not care about this pretty insignificant wrong at the end of my life and I'm better off letting it go. But there have been many times I felt it was important to share my feelings. The Deathbed Gut Check is deeply personal and varies by situation. Your deathbed wisdom might help you see that bringing up a lingering hurt is meaningful to you in the greater scheme of connection with your partner, that it is cultivating vulnerability, or teaching you to stand up for yourself. But using the Deathbed Gut Check could also influence *how* you bring it up, say, with love and compassion instead of anger or disparaging words.

There's almost always a silver lining. A fire claims your home and all your possessions, but you hug your family, grateful that they were spared. You consider taking a lower-paying job that will offer you more time to spend with your family or work on something you are passionate about. Since you are not actually on your deathbed, you might feel gripped with worry or fear about all that you'll have to give up as a result of that decision or whether it's the right choice. But at the moment of death, when everything is stripped away, you'll look back on having lived rich in experience instead of rich in material wealth, and if it aligns for you, you'll feel content.

It's not a perfect technique as we humans are imperfect and constantly growing, learning, becoming more astute in our assessments of what we value and how to align our life to those values. But rather than strive for perfection, we can strive for continuous improvement.

Remember that to die without regret, while not impossible, is wonderfully unlikely. It's wonderful because it releases us from perfection and puts us instead on the course of trying to do our very best. The Deathbed Gut Check is a signal toward the right course, and it can be used again and again to course-correct any time things get hazy along the route.

PART III:

HACK YOUR FEAR OF DEATH

□

CHAPTER 12:

INTRODUCTION TO PART III

After my perspective shifted from living in fear of death to embracing it as my greatest source of inspiration to live, I wondered why no one had told me about this sooner. Was I the first person to have experienced such a revelation? Right, Kate. You're the first ever. Since then, through extensive research, I have discovered that philosophers, great authors, musicians, leaders, and thinkers, all religions, and even your elderly neighbor down the street have also had the same realization. It is highlighted in the earliest work of literature, referenced in the Bible, has entire branches of philosophy and psychology dedicated to studying it, and is the topic of countless modern songs.

It all got me thinking. Why isn't this life hack as common as making vitamins taste like candy? It's simple: fear. So many aspects of death and dying are unknown and the whole thing is so final (scary stuff), and therefore, for the most part, we as individuals and as a society, react as one would to any fear: with avoidance and denial. We avoid thinking about it, live as if it is perpetually in the distant future, categorize it as depressing, and generally minimize our dealings with it as much as possible. But our blind fear of death causes us to throw the baby out with the bathwater. In avoiding death, we avoid real life.

Just as this book — though titled You Might Die Tomorrow

— is actually all about life, so it is with philosophical, religious, and psychological contemplation and commentary on death. Most reflection on death is really a reflection on life. They eat at the same table. And meaning, the intrinsic human desire which separates us from other living species, is always present at that dinner table, quietly lighting the candelabra in the center of the spread. Meaning, Life, and Death all sit and chat animatedly, with a sense of camaraderie. They have much to talk about, they are a trio who influence every human's life, after all. Our relationship with these three comrades is, however, complex.

The exploration of mortality awareness as a profound lifehack is not about eliminating the fear of death. I still fear death. I still occasionally have visions of receiving the call that someone I love has died unexpectedly. I still worry a bit (sometimes more than a bit) that I will regret a decision or chosen path of my life when I die. I'm not going to promise you a future on the other side of this book in which you are freed from all fears surrounding your death because it's not gonna happen. Death is universally scary. Let's just clear that up now. The goal, then, is to accept the reality that we will die, acknowledge the fear that comes with it, and use it as motivation to live a vital, meaningful life.

CHAPTER 13:

OUR DENIAL OF DEATH

"Adults who are racked with death anxiety are not odd birds who have contracted some exotic disease, but men and women whose family and culture have failed to knit the proper protective clothing for them to withstand the icy chill of mortality."
—Irvin D. Yalom, psychiatrist

A Death-Phobic Society

My Grandma Claire and I were very close. I spent many hours of my childhood sitting next to her on the couch in her sunny home while she crocheted or filed her nails, and in her retro kitchen where she taught me how to bake brownies and cakes. On the many sleepovers at Grandma's house, I refused to sleep in the guest room in favor of sleeping on the floor at the foot of her bed. I always felt a deep kinship with her, from as early as I can remember.

She died shortly after I went to college, and when I saw her in the casket at the funeral, she looked waxy and made up. Even the place, a funeral home where I had never been, felt unfamiliar and strange. And with 80 or so people there — many strangers to me — I couldn't sit and be with her for even just a few private moments to tell her how much I loved her and to thank her for being such a special person in my life.

After her death, I saw my favorite film, *Gone with the Wind*, with a new set of eyes. The film is a fictional biopic, based on the book by Margaret Mitchell, about the O'Hara family during the American Civil War. I've watched it roughly a hundred times and I'm always interested in how differently the family treats deaths and mourning than we do today (spoiler alert: many people die). In the film, a newly deceased family member's body is kept in a candlelit room at home for a few days while family members file in and out to keep vigil at the bedside, sometimes for hours at a time.

This is so different from the brief afternoon that Grandma Claire was on display at the crowded funeral home. I wish that I had had that *Gone with the Wind* experience of being able to sit with her for a while, to hold her hand and say my heartfelt goodbye to her in private.

My modern funeral experience is not unusual, but neither was the O'Hara's at the time. Western funeral practices, and even our attitudes toward death and dying, have changed dramatically. First, death was historically more commonplace than it is today. Think back, way back. No plumbing or running water, no vaccines, little understanding of the spread of germs or disease. In 1800s England, life expectancy for males was just 34 years of age. Around that time, one in ten babies died before their first birthday. Death, at all ages, was a frequent part of life.

Throughout the 1900s, however, survival rates grew; the infant mortality rate decreased by ninety percent. Worldwide life expectancy today is around 70 years of age. Today, we see death less frequently. This is a good thing, but it also means that when it happens, we tend to be more shocked and have less experience in how to process it.

Modern death and body care have also changed dramatically. Until the mid-1800s in the United States and Europe, what is usually known as a wake, or viewing of the deceased person, took place in the home as depicted in *Gone With the Wind*. When a person died, the family personally cared for the body and had plenty of time to sit with their loved one. Close members of the family washed and dressed the body. The viewing took place in the front parlor and could last several days until the community procession to the church. It was common for the family to bury the body on their land, where the grave was part of the home and could be visited conveniently.

In the United States, the Civil War brought significant changes to the way people cared for their dead loved ones. With the large number of casualties in that war and the need to ship bodies back to family members, the need arose for preservation during the journey home. Dr. Thomas Holmes was a pioneer of embalming and is said to have embalmed more than 2,000 military men during the war. At $100 per body, it made him a rich man. That set off what is now 'the business of funerals,' with practically all aspects of body care and remembrance services managed (and upsold) by funeral directors at commercial funeral homes.

It should be no surprise that the now multi-billion-dollar funeral industries in the US and Europe have government lobbyists who have successfully changed laws in favor of outsourcing death care and against alternative funeral options. Laws vary by country, state, and region but many restrict who can transport a body, whether a funeral can take place at home, and where a body must be buried. On all counts, cha-ching.

In 2012, the Louisiana State Board of Embalmers and Funeral Directors served a group of Benedictine monks a cease-and-desist order. The monks had begun a small commercial operation selling two models of simple wooden caskets which respectively cost US$1,500 and $2,000. For reference, typical commercial caskets start at $2,000 and can cost $10,000 and beyond. The monks were shocked to learn that there was a law in Louisiana restricting casket sales to licensed funeral directors. They decided to sue to have the law overturned. The case went to the US Supreme Court, and a federal judge ruled in the monks' favor, citing the law's primary purpose as a financial benefit to funeral directors.

Despite this win in Louisiana, funeral homes are still the number one source of corpse and funeral management in Western countries. In short, we outsource and pay for every aspect of the care of our dead.

In the funeral industrial complex, the process is executed with haste. A person dies and their body is quickly taken away. Then, in a foreign place, friends and family have a brief, often crowded opportunity to say our final goodbyes. The body is promptly buried or cremated. And then it's over. In the blink of an eye, it's like the person disappeared and everything is supposed to go back to normal. Most companies offer just three days' bereavement leave for employees, and only for first degree deaths like that of a spouse or child. Can you imagine going back to work just three days after your spouse or child died? How would you feel if your spouse had to go back to work three days after you died? And if your best friend or little niece dies, most employers don't qualify your loss as "primary" enough to qualify for a few days off to grieve.

And then, with a society deeply uncomfortable broaching the topics of death and grief, we mourn alone. While we have Valentine's Day, Mother's Day, and Father's Day, most Western countries have no recurring cultural function dedicated to remembering the people we love who are no longer alive. We also often have difficulty relating to and even judge people who exhibit and speak of grief beyond a short period of time after a death. This has led to a cultural sense that we should just "get over it." A caring check-in as simple as, "How are you doing? How is the grief since your mom died?" is wildly out of the norm. What a shame that we feel too uncomfortable to reach out and acknowledge the grief of someone we love when they may need it most.

Consider how most of us talk about death and dying. I spoke to a woman recently about the benefits of thinking about death regularly. She said she didn't want to think about or mention the 'd' word because she believed it might make her die.

Well, eventually, right?

To be fair, though, isn't it hard to say the word 'died'? Even I, a person who thinks of death regularly and views a healthy awareness of it as profoundly beneficial, often have to force myself away from the well-intended but avoidant turns of phrase like 'passed away' and 'lost,' which have all but replaced plain language like, "my friend died." There's an apt Instagram account called @ theydidntdie, which solely features photos of newspaper obituary clippings that use creative euphemisms for 'died.'

"Nancy moved from her modest home in Mint Hill to a newly prepared mansion in one of Heaven's choicest neighborhoods."

"Samuel played the final note in the long song of his life."

"Jim drank deeply of that bitter cup we must all one day partake."

"It is with heavy hearts that we inform you that Garry peacefully rode into the sunrise early Monday morning."

"Lou and Nel are reunited for their eternal road trip with clean bathrooms at every exit, up front parking at Cracker Barrel and no speeding tickets."

These are at once poetic, endearing, and indicative of our discomfort with acknowledging and talking about death.

The Pursuit of Immortality

Our discomfort with death is not a new phenomenon. As long as humans have been alive, we have grappled with the dilemma of our mortality. What is likely the earliest written work of literature in the world is about — surprise! — avoiding death. *The Epic of Gilgamesh* was written circa 2100 BC on eleven stone slabs. It's about the period in Gilgamesh's life during and after the death of his best friend, Enkidu.

Enkidu was like a brother to Gilgamesh. When he died, Gilgamesh was overcome with agonizing grief. That grief quickly gave rise to an overwhelming fear of his own mortality. Consumed with despair, deep existential questions, and a compulsion to avoid the same mortal fate as his best friend, Gilgamesh set off on a quest to secure immortality. On his quest, Gilgamesh meets Siduri, a woman who lives beside the sea and makes wine. She tells him:

"Gilgamesh, where are you hurrying to? You will never find that life for which you are looking. When the gods created man they allotted to him death, but life they retained in their own keeping.

As for you, Gilgamesh, fill your belly with good things; day and night, night and day, dance and be merry, feast and rejoice. Let your clothes be fresh, bathe yourself in water, cherish the little child that holds your hand, and make your wife happy in your embrace; for this too is the lot of man."

Oh Siduri, how I love your advice. Alas, Gilgamesh ignores her advice. He blindly presses on, despite all his attempts to secure immortality failing. Eventually, he dies exhausted and weathered, having experienced little joy in life. His search for a way to avoid dying consumed him to the point that he wasted the life he had.

History is riddled with examples of the human obsession with immortality. More than 2,000 years ago, the Chinese emperor Qin Shi Huang issued an executive order for a nationwide hunt for an immortality elixir. He literally enlisted all of China to help him never die. But then, fearing that death would find him before his faithful subjects could complete their search, Qin Shi Huang consumed a supposed 'elixir of life' concocted by his own court physicians. It contained high quantities of mercury and he died shortly after drinking it.

Four thousand years since the story of Gilgamesh's fruitless search, we're still trying to hack mortality. From stem cell research to services that will store your body in a deep freeze in hopes that future generations might develop the technology to revive your long-sleeping soul, the modern-day industry for solutions to the death "problem" is big business. Billionaire Peter Thiel has invested tens of millions of dollars in anti-aging research because, in his own words, he is "basically against" death. Today, an anti-aging practice first ideated in the Middle Ages is still in operation and costs around $285,000: young blood transfusions. In this dangerous procedure, older people receive blood and plasma transfusions from those under 25.

Certainly, investing time and money into curing disease has merit. Still, one wonders if some of these vast resources could be better shared with life-enhancing initiatives like education, infrastructure, and palliative care. In a Gilgameshian sprint towards immortality, can one truly appreciate the present reality of mortal life?

Modern Medicine: Live at All Costs

Today, with powerful technology and pharmaceuticals available to extend our lives, those measures are implemented even when it is biologically time to die. A study of 10 developed nations found that one-third of patients over the age of 60 receive invasive and potentially damaging medical treatments in the last six months of their lives, with many extending through the final two weeks. This also means they often spend their last days in a hospital instead of at home.

Only about one-third of American adults have an end-of-life directive of some kind, so doctors and families are often left to make decisions in emotional, intense circumstances. Consider that there are well-published criteria for when to start CPR and which methods to use, but there is no official directive for when to cease. In most cases of medical decision-making, especially without a patient directive, the racked family and obligated doctor cling to life, claw for it, like a cat slipping down the drapes, and choose to do whatever it takes to keep someone from dying. Our doctors, trained and conditioned to keep patients alive, employ save-at-all-costs measures when the chance of survival is low. Often, this results in individuals and families having less time to become accustomed to the real possibility of dying, higher medical costs, and lower quality of life at the end of life.

Eighty percent of Americans at any age die in a hospital or nursing home. This conflicts with polls that show that most Americans say they would prefer to die at home. Modern medicine is built upon what can be done to keep a patient alive and often fails to help a patient and family members decide when it is time to allow the patient to die naturally. We and our families also take a tunnel vision approach to disease: Don't die under any circumstances. But when treatment will be debilitating in its own rite, time-consuming, and expensive, quality of life is sacrificed for quantity of life. For some, that is a fair trade. The problem is that it is rarely a conscious, calculated decision.

It's not all our fault that most of us live in a state of phobic death denial; the fear of death is universal and instinctual. As a result, many cultures have evolved (or, more accurately, devolved) to abstract the notion of death from life. But in our denial of death, we miss the chance to embrace a natural part of life and what it can teach us about how we want to live.

CHAPTER 14:

UNDERSTAND THE FEAR TO OVERCOME IT

So, why is it that most of us live in denial of the reality that we will die, and that it could happen sooner than we assume? It's simple: fear.

Well, actually, not so simple. Fear is a complex bird that requires drive, curiosity, and bravery to confront. Drive because one must possess a desire to confront a fear. Curiosity because the first step in disarming any fear is to better understand it. And bravery because, well, it's scary.

As referenced in the last section, world-renowned spiritual teacher Thich Nhat Hanh encourages people to acknowledge and examine their suffering to experience the transformational benefits of enduring pain. TOMS founder Blake Mycoskie, who often speaks publicly on how to face one's fears, recommends writing down your fears to diminish their power. Something about a fear's limitless and shape-shifting nature in our mind makes it more terrifying. Once on paper, a fear often loses some of its frightening mystique and feels more manageable.

According to Blake's and Thich's teachings, then, the first step is to acknowledge your fear and the next step is to better understand it. The first part is up to you. Now is a great moment to take a calming breath and say to yourself, *"I don't want to die.*

I am afraid of dying. And that's okay."

As for the second step, to better understand the human fear of dying, all you have to do, with even a speck of drive, curiosity, and bravery, is to read this chapter.

This chapter explores the psychology of how humans respond to our mortal fears and explains a great deal about how we live. Next, we get to reap the benefits of our work. Chapter 15 will show you how to use your fear of death as motivation to live your best life. I believe you have the drive, curiosity, and bravery to confront your fear of death, and on the other side, find your greatest motivation to really live while you're alive.

The Worm at the Core

There are so many aspects of death that frighten us. It's unsettling that it's unknown in that we don't know how or when we will die, but also that humanity and science have little knowledge of what the dying experience is like. We're afraid that it could be painful or scary, and that it may come unexpectedly. We fear that we will leave behind the people we love, and we feel sad that our death will create pain for others. We fear that we may not have lived well or meaningfully while we were alive. Since all we've ever known is existing, even the very notion that we will expire and no longer exist is frightening.

Ernest Becker is a PhD in cultural anthropology who, in his younger years as a professor, kept getting fired from his jobs at prominent universities for standing up for his beliefs, particularly freedom. I love his work because he takes a macro, multidisciplinary approach to understanding humanity, scientifically informed but unbound by only scientific explanations. After all, why should concepts as complex and heady as the nature of human consciousness and the meaning of life be explained only from a psychological standpoint, or only from an anthropological perspective, without acknowledging that science hasn't yet explained everything? Becker took a step back, way back, and drew together research from philosophy, psychology, anthropology, religion, and science to explore what makes us humans live as we live. He put his analysis and conclusions into a book, *The Denial of Death.*

That book won the Pulitzer Prize in 1974. Its conclusion? As narcissistic creatures, humans naturally fear the reality of mortality (or nonexistence) and our innate fear of death is the greatest influence on human behavior. He asserts that everything humans do stems from the basic drive to assuage the fear of death. He quotes William James, who calls death the "worm at the core" of the human condition.

Later, three psychologists heavily influenced by Becker's work — Sheldon Solomon, Jeff Greenberg, and Tom Pyszczynski — further dug into the psychological root of *why* we're so afraid of death. It's like this: We humans have an innate self-preservation instinct. This natural survival instinct is at odds with our cognitive awareness that our survival efforts will ultimately prove futile. This paradox freaks us out.

The fear of death is, after all, different from all other fears: It is unsurvivable. No matter what we do in life to stay alive, we will eventually die. This produces a "basic psychological conflict" which causes anxiety and, in some cases, terror.

Becker says the base-level fear of not existing influences significantly how we live, both consciously and subconsciously. He says we manage this terror by, I'll paraphrase, *doin' stuff* in life that makes us feel better. As an example, I think it's like my anxious habit of compulsively buying stuff. If I'm getting sick, I'll frantically hit up Walgreens pharmacy and throw money at the problem to make myself feel like I'm *doing something* about it.

But Becker believes that our symbolic death-defying actions go far beyond a few bottles of cough syrup. He thinks everything — and I mean every conscious and subconscious expression of humanity and human culture — stems from our fear of dying and our desire to transcend that expiration.

Yes, all of it: political systems, culture, social media, war, procreation, religion, art, fame. He calls them our "immortality projects," and posits that all of them can be tied back to our existential dread, to "reaching out of one's whole being toward life." We are aware we cannot physically transcend mortality, but our drive to live (and our drive to not die) pushes us to strive to transcend mortality *symbolically*.

Becker concludes *The Denial of Death* with the idea that all of this is perfectly okay. His decades of research and thought led him to believe that acknowledging death and trying to create meaning is the best way to live. He says, "whatever man does on this planet has to be done in the lived truth of the terror of creation, of the grotesque, of the rumble of panic underneath everything."

Death is scary. Full stop. One can succumb to the terror of it, or one can acknowledge the fear and use it to create vibrant life.

Ways We Manage the Fear of Death:
Symbolic Immortality

Humans predominantly react to fear through self-protection. The automatic, internal responses to threat and danger are fight, flight, or freeze. The thing is, death is as yet unable to be ultimately fled or fought off. And to freeze or become paralyzed in response to the fear does nothing to negate the threat.

The futility of self-protecting against death, however, doesn't really stop our persistent attempts to fight, flee, or freeze. We discussed in the last chapter some of the many ways humans try to circumvent death, such as seeking physical immortality or attempting to extend life at all costs. But behaviors to preserve life can be beneficial. One way we flee our finitude is taking care of our health and safety. This is the *"I know I'll die eventually, but I want to avoid it for as long as possible"* by wearing sunscreen and not petting a grizzly bear stuff.

We also "fight" against death by prolonging the life of our name and essence. The idea of "symbolic immortality" was coined by social psychiatrist Robert Jay Lifton a few years before Becker's book was published. It is the idea that, although our physical bodies will die, we can achieve immortality through what remains of our life after our death. In simple terms, we want to live forever, but we can't, so while we're alive, we strive to do things that we think will ensure that our name or essence lives on forever.

We all leverage symbolic immortality in one way or another, and it produces lots of positive results. Both Becker and Lifton acknowledge the healthy, productive nature of our symbolic immortality projects and the benefit of meaning they bring to our existence. And unlike literal immortality, symbolic immortality is actually possible, and it *makes us feel better about dying*. These are the raid-the-cold-medicine-section-at-Walgreens comfort strategies to quell those fires of fear of nonexistence that always live within us. Lifton has categorized these strategies into biologic, religious, creative, natural, and transcendent modes of symbolic immortality.

1. Biologic

Having kids is one way humans strive for symbolic immortality. The motivation is twofold. First, producing offspring ensures a physical legacy. Part of a parent's DNA is contained in their offspring and often passed down through generations. A similar phenomenon applies to organ donation. A part of the deceased donor lives on in the recipient. This almost always makes the family of the deceased person feel that something productive has come from their loss and that a piece of the person they love lives on.

Second, having children increases the likelihood that one's name and story will be known after one's death. Have you ever envisioned a comforting scene in which you sit in a rocking chair on the porch with a gaggle of young grandchildren at your feet? Perhaps they hop onto your lap as you tell them stories about your life and share your lessons on how to live well. These small, young humans know you and your life, and they have so much life ahead of them. They will remember your name and may tell your story, which could be told and retold for many generations.

All of this eases the blow of knowing that we will cease

to exist, so we pursue procreation as a symbolic life-extending measure.

2. Religion and/or belief in the afterlife

The fact that the experience of life after death is unknown can be scary. Better, then, to imagine we don't *really* die, that we go on forever in a utopian place where everything is dreamy and wonderful and perfect, or that we get to turn around and come back to life as something else. Sounds good, right? It certainly does to billions of religious people all around the world. Most religious beliefs subscribe to death transcendence, or an afterlife. A majority of religious teachings provide answers to the great questions of life and ease fears about dying.

In fact, studies show that intrinsically religious people tend to show less death anxiety than non-religious or "superficially" religious people. Religion — in particular a belief in reincarnation or the afterlife — makes humans feel better about dying by offering a path to symbolic immortality.

3. Creativity or achievements in life

Writing this book has been one of the most emotionally challenging experiences of my life. It's an ongoing battle with my ego. Who am I to write a book? Does anyone care about this stuff? Haven't ancient philosophers already written about these topics? Is my writing any good?

So, why have I obstinately persevered through these dark nights of the soul? Partly because I believe passionately in the message and want to help others live more authentically. But also because I love the idea of having written a book. It's so tangible, so real. My name is printed on the front! Even if a time comes when not many people care about it, the book will still exist. It will live on, even when I don't. My name and words will be recorded in history. I'll have a little piece of immortality.

A driving motivation to achieve and create in life comes from our desire to be remembered as great. Being featured in a more lasting medium than the human body (film, music, canvas, page, hall of fame) or in the memories of others through great work (teaching, medicine, philanthropy) lends immortality to our name and essence.

4. Nature

The lifespan of a human is minuscule compared to the lifespan of a mountain, a river, or of the earth itself. And yet, as organic matter ourselves, we are a part of nature's great cycle of persistent birth and death.

Our engagement with nature brings about feelings of symbolic immortality by reminding us that we are a part of something more lasting than ourselves.

In life, we cultivate this sense of natural symbolic immortality by engaging with nature. We use nature as a source of spiritual refreshment and to experience awe. We feel that we have contributed to the cycle by planting a tree that may live long beyond our own lives. Even protecting nature through an ecologically-minded lifestyle might be attributed to a desire for the world we know, love, and lived in to be experienced by future generations. And, even in death, the notion that our bodies go back to the cycle of nature brings us comfort.

5. Transcendent experience

This fifth and final mode of symbolic immortality is quite different than the other four. It's not something we do, it's an experience of being.

In transcendent experience, we feel we transcend our base existence and enter a realm in which we forget about death and time and enter a state of transcendent flow. Within this state, we feel we 'go beyond' the limits of everyday life. Afterward, our sense of meaning and/or priorities in life are changed.

Transcendent experience can be experienced *within* the other four modes of symbolic immortality, such as through moments of profound love for our kids, being recognized for a great achievement, or an experience of awe in nature. Other ways humans have experienced transcendence include meditation and mindfulness, childbirth, orgasm, friendship, love, and drug-induced psychedelic experiences, among many others. I believe calm reflection on the reality that one will die can produce a transcendent experience of feeling profoundly alive.

Our attempts at symbolic immortality are beautiful. Ego-driven as they may be, they exist because we love life. Our innate survival instinct propels us to propagate life, in any form, with everything we've got. That's what's remarkable: this animal instinct to stay alive has given way to a complex and profound system of values and beliefs which make us *feel good about our lives and fear death less.* We've responded to an internal call for self-preservation with books, companies, humanitarian work, faith in higher powers, babies, and the pursuit of the experience of awe. In the absence of knowing really what the hell we're doing here, we've created a world in which we can matter.

The Human Drive to Matter

We've already looked at many of the reasons humans fear death and desire immortality. We've established that the fear of death is universal and that we manage that fear through immortality projects. But why do humans even desire immortality? On the surface, it's easy to see that we have a desire to live forever both because dying is scary and because we don't want our experience to end. But by looking even deeper, we can discover what innately drives us.

Becker posits that, as a result of the childhood experience of having all our needs catered to and often being the center of attention, humans are narcissistic to a degree. In adulthood, we feel a pressure to craft our lives toward personal success and recognition as a result of our childhood conditioning. We have a profound desire to be seen for all that we are.

This is the root of our desire for immortality and our fear of dying: the desire to *matter and to be seen*. It's based on the nature of self-esteem, which is our key weapon in the fight to feel good and assert ourselves in life. Terror management theory (TMT) research shows that humans consistently draw upon our symbolic systems of meaning and value, which are related to a sense of self-esteem, as a coping mechanism for dealing with our fear of death. Here are some examples.

A group of psychologists testing terror management theory at the University of Arizona in 2016 facilitated a study that linked awareness of mortality to superior athletic performance. They wanted to understand whether there is a link between existential concerns and one's motivation to excel, in this case in sports.

The subjects were male college students who indicated they played and enjoyed basketball and cared about their playing performance. The first study was built around one-on-one games against one of the study investigators who was posing as another subject. They played the first game, then completed either a questionnaire about death or about basketball. Then, they returned to the court for a second game. Those who completed the death questionnaire improved their performance in the second game by 40 percent. Those asked about basketball saw no change in performance.

A second study showed similar results using different circumstances. The researchers looked at how participants performed in an individual basket-shooting challenge when presented with a subtle reminder of death. This time, instead of a questionnaire about death, the variable was the ref's attire. The ref wore a black t-shirt with a skull and the word 'death' when refereeing the test group. For the control group, he zipped up his jacket to hide the skull and death design.

Participants who saw the skull shirt outperformed those who did not by approximately 30 percent. They also attempted more shots, an average of 11.85 per minute versus 8.33 by those who did not see the shirt.

This study shows a strong correlation between thinking

about death and improving performance. But other studies which engaged subjects in an activity they did not find meaningful did not yield the same positive performance. This has led to the generally accepted conclusion among TMT researchers that thinking about death doesn't make us better at everything we do, but it does have the potential to make us perform better in activities which have meaning to us.

The reason these individuals' basketball-playing performance improved in response to the mortality cue is because their self-esteem was related to their playing abilities. They doubled down on that form of self-protecting self-esteem as a way to manage the emotions and fears brought up by thinking of death.

So, what happens, then, when we are faced with a death cue while *not* engaged in a personally meaningful activity? We still grasp for meaning and self-esteem as a form of self-protection, but the self-esteem comes from a different source.

We tend to think of self-esteem as how highly we think of our authentic selves. But we are also conditioned to draw self-esteem from culturally approved, extrinsic sources like financial wealth, power, status, physical attractiveness, and our sense of belonging to a group. So whether you get a sense of self-esteem from being American, believing in God, having a lot of money, performing expert brain surgery, being kind, or having strong basketball playing skills, it is your personal constellation of values — from both intrinsic and extrinsic sources — which informs how you respond to the awareness that you will die.

Consider the polarized responses after the September 11, 2001 terrorist attacks in the US. Following the event, there was a rise in incidences of 'ordinary' Americans who, threatened by the events, committed unjust violent acts against people they perceived to be terrorists. This phenomenon can be classified as a disturbing example of people leveraging self-esteem in response to fear. In this case, the self-esteem is derived by clinging more tightly to a social group.

Conversely, many people responded to that same threat with humanitarianism. Applications to 'helping' professions such as teaching, firefighting, and health care soared after the attacks. Applications to Teach for America, for example, tripled, with half of the new applicants specifically attributing their decision to pursue teaching to the events of September 11.

In response to a very real reminder of mortality — a national tragedy — some people reacted with violence and others with benevolence. Why? Because the way we react to our fear of death depends on the beliefs and values from which we source our self-esteem.

Those who reacted with violence leaned on a self-aggrandizing sense of belonging to American culture. Those who reacted with altruistic benevolence, on the other hand, leaned on their intrinsic desire to create meaning through helping others, or perhaps on their desire for symbolic immortality through personal achievement. Our "constellation of beliefs and values" inform so many of our behaviors in life, including how we respond to the notion of our mortality.

CHAPTER 15:

HOW TO HACK YOUR FEAR OF DEATH TO LIVE YOUR MOST MEANINGFUL LIFE

Let's put all of this research together. By better understanding the ways we humans deal with our mortal reality and the fear that comes along with that, we now have the opportunity to use that information to our benefit. That life ends and that it's scary to humans can be used productively to create one's most authentic and meaningful expression of life.

Step 1: Acknowledge that death is scary. Make friends with it anyway.

The first step to making your fear of death productive is to acknowledge that death and fear are inextricable. The ideas of dying and nonexistence will always be scary to some degree. We're human and dying is scary. Fred Rogers, better known as *Mr. Rogers*, reassures us that "anything that's human is mentionable, and anything that is mentionable can be more manageable." Elizabeth Gilbert creates a perfect metaphor for how she manages the constant nature of fear: a road trip. Since fear is always on the "road trip," part of the human experience, she tells fear to get in the backseat and sets the ground rules: *"You're not allowed to touch the road maps; you're not allowed to suggest detours; you're not allowed to fiddle with the temperature. Dude, you're not even allowed to touch the radio. But above all else, my dear old familiar friend, you are absolutely forbidden to drive."*

I let the fear of death drive my life for a year. During that year, I spoke about it to no one, and as a result, the fear had nowhere to go. So it grew and took stronger root within me. Like Mr. Rogers said, "mentioning" our fears makes them more manageable. This is why facing your fear of death is the other non-negotiable part of disarming it and making it your friend.

I recently holed up to write for three days in a trailer in the Chihuahuan desert in West Texas. While I wouldn't call myself a "city" woman, I was certainly not the rattlesnake-lassoing ranch lady I hoped I'd be out there. When I entered the outhouse the first night to find a large, oddly translucent scorpion hanging out in the sink, I basically levitated from the floor and sprang backwards through the door. That scorpion, however, didn't move an inch from its trusty water source for the duration of my stay. What changed was my response. As the days went on and I repeatedly encountered the creature, I became cool with it. He didn't bother me; I didn't bother him. I could just pee while he chilled in the sink. Eventually, I even began to see how interesting a creature it was. Repeated exposure to my fear reduced it to a manageable level and allowed me to see the thing I was afraid of with clear, adrenaline-free eyes.

We can actually "rewire" our brains and change our response to a fear through exposure therapy. By actively choosing to expose oneself to a fear, you can mentally prepare for it, improving your chances of a more positive response. As you continue to calmly approach your fear and repeatedly experience more positive responses, you recondition your brain's fear response to it.

If you're afraid of heights, for example, a therapist might recommend you ascend a bit higher in a building each week, becoming more and more comfortable until you are able to stand on the roof and peek over the edge without having an anxiety attack. Eventually, you might find yourself casually leaning against the handrail of a rooftop bar on the 22nd floor as you tell a hilarious story to a group of rapt friends. It's the same for the fear of death. Consistently push yourself to face your fear in gentle, mindful ways and you may find that, eventually, it is largely replaced with a calm awareness of a natural fact of life.

Step 2: Enjoy your life

In Chapter 14, we explored the concept that humans rely on self-esteem to manage our fear of death. When confronted with a reminder of mortality, our natural reaction is to assert ourselves through meaningful action, like those who flocked to helping professions after 9/11. As a result, more recent and advanced studies on the effects of mortality awareness on human behavior explore the positive, prosocial effects.

A great example is Matthew Gailliot's 2008 study which tested whether being near a cemetery impacted people's willingness to help a stranger. In the study, researchers controlled for a mortality cue and an opportunity for meaningful action. Researchers placed actors either in front of a cemetery or on an ordinary street corner two blocks away. At both locations, one actor would first engage a participant in a conversation about the value of helping strangers. Then, a few moments after the participant walked away, another actor would struggle with her backpack and drop her notebook in their path. The study found that 40% more participants in front of the cemetery picked up the notebook than at the other location.

You might wonder why the researchers first engaged the participants in a conversation specifically about the value of egalitarianism. The reason is because for the experiment to work, they needed to ensure that helping others was made salient as a positive value to the participants. The is because death reminders don't necessarily make people do nice things or behave better. Rather, mortality awareness makes people adhere more tightly to personal or cultural values.

Think back to that basketball study. The players who had death on the brain worked harder and performed better because their basketball skills were a meaningful avenue to being awesome in life before death. One could infer, then, that the subjects would have displayed improved performance whether it was a basketball competition, *RuPaul's Drag Race*, or a thumb war, *as long as the subject of competition had meaning to them*. What matters to us creates meaning, and what has meaning helps us manage our fear of death.

Let's widen our scope and apply this phenomenon to life. If a person finds meaning in living a "good" life, then doing so can make them feel better about dying. Because self-esteem is a natural anxiety buffer, if we have the sense that we are doing awesomely in life, we *feel better about dying*.

This is important. What constitutes a "good" life is highly subjective to the individual. To get the fear-reducing benefits of living meaningfully, you must have a sense of what is actually meaningful to you. If you aren't quite sure yet, fear not. The exercises in the next section will help you tap into your most meaningful priorities. And remember that we're all just taking a best guess. The idea of living each day meaningfully may feel daunting. I find it easier, then, to strive to *enjoy my life and have fun every day.* I figure that if I am really enjoying myself along the way, I'm living in a way that fulfills me, has meaning to me, and that I will feel good about when it comes time to look back.

In Summary: How to Hack Your Fear of Death to Live Your Most Meaningful Life

1. Acknowledge that death is scary and cultivate a gentle awareness of mortality in your everyday life.
2. Actively live meaningfully.

Thinking about death motivates you to live more in alignment with your values and living in alignment with your values makes you less afraid of dying. It's a complementary circular reference, my friends! To minimize the fear of death, live a meaningful life.

In the event a human encounters an aggressive bear, that person has some options: run away, run toward it to fight it, or stand to face it. If the person chooses the option to run away, the bear is very likely to give chase, catch the human, and rip 'em to shreds. If one decides to charge and fight the bear, the chances of winning are meager. So, those running and fighting ideas, not really recommended. In a bear aggression or attack situation, most bear safety experts agree that the best tactic is to calmly face the bear and make yourself as formidable an opponent as possible. Stand on a rock, raise and wave your arms, and loudly yell, "Hey, bear!"

And so it is with our fear of death: we can attempt to run away from our certain mortality, we can try to fight it by living cautiously or seeking immortality, or we can bravely face it and live formidably before we die. We have the choice of how to respond to the reality of our mortality. Our only effective form of self-protection against death — an unsurvivable threat — is to valiantly face it and fight instead for a formidable life.

PART IV:

HOW TO FACE DEATH AND FIND YOUR MEANINGFUL THINGS

CHAPTER 16:

INVITE DEATH AWARENESS INTO YOUR LIFE

Thinking about death reminds you to live. If you want to wake up to this life-changing way of living, you can take the long road and wait for external events to influence your perspective and fear response to death like I did. Some of the external life events that can trigger a new perspective or awareness of death include the death of someone we know, a birthday (particularly round age numbers), a reunion, or an injury or near-death experience. Or, you can take the proactive approach and integrate a sustained practice of death awareness into your life.

This chapter highlights some examples of a more positive, everyday awareness of death, followed by some suggestions for how you can actively pursue death awareness to change your life for the better.

Alternatives to Death Denial: Death Awareness in Philosophy, Religion, and Culture

Among philosophers, death has always been a key topic. Arthur Schopenhauer famously called death the "muse of philosophy." In Stoicism, a major school of philosophy founded around the 3rd century B.C., the path to a good, happy life is to concern oneself with what is within one's control and disregard the rest. This is how the Stoicists subdued their fear of death: by accepting it as a universal reality one cannot change and thus, resolving to not waste time worrying about it. That doesn't mean they forgot about death. On the contrary, they regularly practiced memento mori, or remembrance of death, and they heralded an awareness of death as the greatest motivation to make the most of one's life.

Well-known Stoicist Marcus Aurelius said, "It is not death that a man should fear, but he should fear never beginning to live." Their view was that actions and time are the elements of our lives most within our control and, therefore, humans' most valuable resources. Seneca noted that we can be tight-fisted with our money, but that we think little of the value of time and often waste that most precious resource. The Stoics used a death-aware mindset to revere the present moment and the gift of life.

"When you arise in the morning think of what a privilege it is to be alive, to think, to enjoy, to love."
—Marcus Aurelius

Religion is rife with exhortations to be aware of one's mortality. In Buddhism, *The Five Remembrances* are the five facts of life that must be reflected upon for a good life.

1. I am of the nature to grow old. There is no way to escape growing old.
2. I am of the nature to have ill health. There is no way to escape ill health.
3. I am of the nature to die. There is no way to escape death.
4. All that is dear to me and everyone I love are of the nature to change. There is no way to escape being separated from them.
5. My actions are my only true belongings. I cannot escape the consequences of my actions. My actions are the ground upon which I stand.

Maranasati is the term for the range of Buddhist practices relating to meditating on the nature of death. These practices include everything from meditating on the Five Remembrances, to observing one's breath as a symbol of life, to seeking exposure to external death reminders like looking at skeletons or images of skeletons and visiting cemeteries.

Sogyal Rinpoche is a Tibetan Buddhist who wrote the world-famous *The Tibetan Book of Living and Dying* based on *The Tibetan Book of the Dead.* Here is his advice on how to improve one's relationship with death:

"Reflecting on death needn't be frightening or morbid. Why not reflect on death when you are really inspired, relaxed, and comfortable, lying in bed, or on holiday, or listening to music that particularly delights you? Why not reflect on it when you are happy, in good health, confident, and full of well-being?"

Christianity, too, has plenty of mortality reminders. The expression memento mori itself is attributed to the Christians. And then there's the dead Jesus statue front and center at just about every Catholic church in the world. I appreciate this wisdom from the Bible in Ecclesiastes: "For death is the destiny of everyone; the living should take this to heart."

If you travel to Rome, head toward Our Lady of the Conception of the Capuchins. Beneath the church, you can tour the ossuary crypt, a chapel housing the bones of nearly 4,000 friars. Thousands of human skulls and hundreds of thousands of bones hang from the walls and ceiling, many arranged into ornate murals and others as full skeletons standing upright wearing traditional friar robes. Though physically underground, this was not a fringe effort. Pope Urban III oversaw the construction of the crypt and it was used by the brothers of the Capuchin order as a place of prayer and reflection. The Catholic Order has stated that it is not meant to be macabre, but rather a reminder of our short life and mortality.

Another example still practiced today in Catholic churches around the world is Ash Wednesday. Ash Wednesday is the holy day in which Catholics go to church in the middle of the week to have a priest rub a cross in black ash on their third eye (ahem, forehead) as a public display of faith and reminder of mortality. As the forehead is anointed with ash, the priest says, "Remember that you are dust, and to dust you shall return."

Many cultures have mortality awareness practices. The people of Bhutan — who, by the way, are widely considered to be the happiest population in the world — have a practice of thinking about death five times per day. Their belief is that "to be a truly happy person, one must think about death five times per day." The people of Bhutan take these regular opportunities throughout daily life to reflect on death and accept it as a part of the greater cycle of existence, believing it provides a necessary realignment between the struggles of daily life and the ideals of greater meaning.

In Malaysia, every five to seven years, people remove their family members' bodies from their crypts and reclothe them for the evening's party in which the corpses are danced with to live music. The Malaysians call this their *famadihana* tradition, or "turning of the bones."

Too dusty for you? In New Orleans, parades are a typical part of funerals, and everyone is invited to participate. The funeral procession might start somberly, but after the body is laid to rest in the cemetery, the march turns raucous and merry with jazz music and dancing. As any and all passersby are encouraged to join the dancing street parade, you could be walking to the corner store on an ordinary day and end up dancing in celebration of the life of a stranger.

Perhaps the most widely known cultural celebration of death is México's *El Día de los Muertos*, now popularized around the world by Disney's film Coco and other cinematic and commercial retail interpretations. For all the Día de los Muertos tchotchkes I see in the seasonal aisle at my local Austin grocery store, the true Día de Muertos in México is a private family affair. It's a multiday holiday to remember and celebrate loved ones who have died, generally celebrated from October 31 to November 2. It includes Día de los Muertos, celebrating the souls of all deceased loved ones, as well as *Día de los Inocentes* to celebrate dead children (also referred to as *Día de los Angelitos*).

Together, families visit their loved ones' graves, cleaning them up and creating *ofrendas*, similar to an altar, decorated with photos, treats, and marigold flowers. On the celebratory nights, they sing songs and share poems that include often funny anecdotes about the dead family members' personalities.

These traditions help the living process their grief and serve as a comfort that they, too, will be remembered after they die. Día de los Muertos is, functionally, an effective way to manage fears of death, the mystery of the afterlife, and the pain and sadness of grief.

A more open and accepting attitude toward death is beginning to evolve in Western culture. This evolution can be seen in the growing popularization of celebrations of life, home funerals, and embalming and burial alternatives like cremation. In the US today, cremation is the choice for 54% of people, up from just 5% in 1970. My boss Stephen's memorial service closed with a fireworks show. As of 2014, the most popular funeral song choice in the UK is Monty Python's "Always Look on the Bright Side of Life."

Just the other day, I stumbled upon a product online called The Cuddle Cot. The product's tagline: "The Cuddle Cot gives grieving parents the gift of time." It's a baby basket system lined with a cooling pad that allows parents to stay with their deceased baby longer, either in the hospital or at home, before the body is moved to the morgue or funeral home. What a beautiful modern invention that bucks the norm.

In 2016, the story of 91-year old Norma Bauerschmidt was shared and reshared around the world. Norma was faced with doctors' recommendations of surgery, chemotherapy, and radiation to *hopefully* cure her Stage IV uterine mass. Instead, she chose to take herself and her uterine mass on an incredible adventure traveling around the country with her adult kids and dog in an RV. What a badass, right? I think the most badass part of this story is that Norma had the wisdom and chutzpah to recognize that her life was ending and chose her own adventure for her last days. Norma's story went viral because her story of breaking from the herd resonated with people.

These are just a fraction of the examples of creative and comforting ways humans have found to maintain a healthy and productive awareness of mortality in life.

Ways To Face Your Fear of Death and Integrate Mortality Awareness into Your Life

To think differently about the way we handle death means we must actually think about death. Here are some ways you can incorporate the practice of mortality awareness into your life.

Actively seek out content on the topic. Here are some examples of "external" mortality reminders and death-positive content.

- **App:** Download the WeCroak app to your device, which sends you a "don't forget, you're going to die" notification five times per day (inspired by the Bhutanese practice).
- **Podcasts:** *Death in the Afternoon* by Caitlin Doughty, *Live Like You Are Dying* by Fi Munro, Ph.D, *The Death Dialogues Project* by Becky Aud-Jennison, *End-of-Life University* by

Dr. Karen Wyatt, *The Adventures of Memento Mori* by D.S. Moss

- **Music:** Follow the You Might Die Tomorrow playlist on Spotify, which has three hours of inspiring, death-aware music (please message me online if you have a song suggestion!).
- **Films:** *Extremis* (documentary; get your tissues ready), *The Bucket List* (comedy), *Up* (animated), *Coco* (animated), *American Beauty* (drama), *My Girl* (drama), *Amour* (drama), *Alternate Endings* (documentary), *End Game* (documentary)
- **Books:** *Staring at the Sun* by Dr. Irvin D. Yalom, *Man's Search for Meaning* by Viktor Frankl, *When Breath Becomes Air* by Paul Kalanithi, *Dying to be Me* by Anita Moorjani, *The Tibetan Book of Living and Dying* by Sogyal Rinpoche
- **Instagram accounts and hashtags:** @youmightdietomorrow, @whenyoudie_org, @talkdeathdaily, @deathafternoon, @rememberyoudie, #impermanence, #mementomori, #deathpositive
- **Products:** You Might Die Tomorrow reminder products (self-promo alert; available on my website), The Death Deck conversation card game, Hello Game conversation deck
- **Events:** Reimagine Festival in NYC and LA, Death Café (global, ongoing), Death over Dinner (global, ongoing)
- **Actions:** Arrange your end-of-life affairs including your Advanced Directive, Will, and your wishes regarding your remains and your funeral or memorial. You may find that having your affairs in order reduces the (very common) fear of being a burden to those you love or leaving loose ends behind.

An integrated, personal awareness of mortality in life is the ideal to strive toward. Cultivate this by calmly and thoughtfully noticing elements of ending and mortality in your everyday life:

- When things around you die or come to an end (plants, events, moods, etc.), thoughtfully notice and strive to come to peace with those endings.
- As you have fears that come up concerning death and dying, write them down. Writing down fears often diminishes their power and can make you feel better and more in control.
- Talk to people about death and dying.
  - If someone you know has a terminal illness, ask them how they feel about the idea of dying. You will likely find they are grateful to have someone to talk about their feelings with, and that the discussion makes you more comfortable with the idea of dying, too.
  - If someone you know is grieving, call them up or shoot them a text and ask them how their grief has been lately and what it's like. Or, if you knew the person who died, let them know that you think about the person and/or share a story about them.
- Try out using the word "died" instead of "lost" or other euphemisms.
- Use the awareness of not knowing when you will die as your motivation to appreciate the present moment.
- Use the Deathbed Gut Check from Chapter 11 as an everyday way to use your mortality to help you make tough decisions in life.

- Do the Deathbed Meditation in Chapter 18 from time to time to become more comfortable with dying and to gain insight into how you'd like to live.

The Bhutanese who think about death five times per day are human just like the rest of us; they, too, fear death. But in repeatedly confronting it, studying it, and seeing what it has to teach us, the fear shrinks in the light and becomes instead a source which illuminates your vision of an authentic life.

CHAPTER 17:

LIVE IN ALIGNMENT
WITH YOUR MEANING

This last part of the book helps you better understand the concept of living meaningfully and offers exercises to help you discover your true priorities in life and how close — or far off — you are from living in alignment with them.

Purpose vs. Meaning

Before the exercises, let's get one thing straight: this chapter is not necessarily about finding your single great purpose in life. Trying to find one's single great purpose in life has the dangerous potential to create undue pressure and inspire decision paralysis. Meaning, on the other hand, is something that can be sought and cultivated in every moment of every day. Purpose is an action; meaning is a state of mind.

The phrase 'you might die tomorrow' is a call to remind you to live in the present moment. If we only have today, we should chiefly concern ourselves with finding meaning and feeling good about what we are doing today. It's less about seeking one single purpose and more about cultivating a sense of gratification from the way we live and spend our Life Time and energy.

Meaning in Our Lives

Viktor Frankl is a psychiatrist, neurologist, and Holocaust survivor. He is the founder of logotherapy, a psychological therapy modality based on the concept that, rather than avoiding death or pursuing power or pleasure, striving to find meaning in life is the primary, most powerful motivating and driving force in humans. Frankl's fundamental principles of logotherapy:

- Life has meaning under all circumstances, even the most miserable ones.
- Our main motivation for living is our will to find meaning in life.
- We have freedom to find meaning in what we do, and what we experience, or at least in the stance we take when faced with a situation of unchangeable suffering.

The majority of Frankl's personal and professional work on human meaning occurred during his horrific internment and after his liberation from Nazi death camps during World War II. His traumatic experience, however, is what helped him see that meaning can come from suffering. Frankl's three main avenues through which one arrives at meaning in life:

1. By creating a work or doing a deed
2. By experiencing something or encountering someone
3. By the attitude we take toward unavoidable suffering

Creating something or meeting someone sound like much more enjoyable pathways to meaning than a personal tragedy. However, suffering is often the most available avenue; we usually have some form of suffering in our life at any given time. Frankl's theory helps us see that the very act of choosing an attitude of growth in the face of our suffering can be a source of meaning.

One can derive meaning from work, engaging in pleasurable activities, connecting with nature, taking calculated risks, enjoying the moment, and learning from an experience. One can feel meaningfully fulfilled from interactions such as saying hello to neighbors, spending time with family, engaging with strangers, and helping others in small ways. One could view the fear of death as a form of suffering and, therefore, an opportunity for growth.

Your Meaningful Things can be anything. They don't need to win you any awards or make you millions of dollars. They are different for everyone. That's the point: Your meaningful things are a reflection of what's meaningful to *you*. Not to your parents, your boss, and not what *you* think your parents and boss think are meaningful. Meaningful Things are simply actions or states of being in life which align to your core personal values and make you feel fulfilled.

Big Meaningful Things and Small Meaningful Things

Big Meaningful Things are sweeping life actions. Things like quitting a job; starting a business; having, adopting, or fostering kids; taking a big trip; forgiving a family member; and on and on. You'll know they're big if they kinda freak you out.

Small Meaningful Things, on the other hand, are everyday actions and practices. Some examples of Small Meaningful Things: regularly appreciating nature, making sure the people you love know you love them, spending time with those people, being a positive influence to other humans with whom you cross paths, taking time to engage in an activity which brings you joy, and taking at least one moment each day to really feel and enjoy being alive.

Those sound pretty big, I know. But I consider them Small Meaningful Things because they only require small, everyday actions to fulfill. It's slowing down, showing up for friends and family, listening to people with undivided attention, helping the little old lady cross the street type stuff. Small Meaningful Things are only small in the sense that they are everyday actions. They are of great importance.

Small micro-actions and shifts in perspective make up our greater sense of satisfaction in life. Sure, the big stuff gets all the attention, but while big stuff can be invigorating and life-affirming, that exhilaration fades. Big stuff is effective, but rare. Life gratification comes from opening oneself to the everyday joys of being alive.

That the little stuff can be profoundly meaningful doesn't mean we shouldn't have big goals and dreams. But it would be a tragedy to focus on those at the expense of the profound impact we can have in the pursuit of the little ways we can show up for ourselves and those around us along the way.

To make any Big or Small Meaningful Things happen, you've got to do two things.

One: Choose an attitude to approach your life with. Actively choose the energy you want to bring to life and it will influence every action you take, big and small. It may also become your calling card in life and part of your legacy after you die. Do you want to be a cheerful person? A person that makes people laugh? Someone who always encourages others? A great listener? The person who always helps the underdog? Pick one. It helps to stick with one specific approach; it doesn't mean you won't also engage in other ways, but it's easier and more productive to have a single-minded goal.

Me? My goal is to approach life with excited curiosity. In turn, this helps me show up in my daily life in a way that is meaningful to me. It inspires me to get to know the clerk at my corner store, to really listen and learn when in conversation with someone, and to get really excited on the birthday of people I love so they feel special.

Our life is made up of millions, if not billions, of individual, everyday experiences. While I would love to be remembered for writing a book that changed the lives of millions of people, I recognize that my best chance at making a profound impact on this world comes in my attitude in my daily interactions with the humans around me.

Two: To live meaningfully, you'll have to actually do things in life which are meaningful to you. It will not always be easy or fun. Here is where the rubber meets the road. To be a blessing to everyone you cross paths with, you'll have to smile at the guy that cuts you off in traffic. Making sure the people you love know you love them means you'll have to do so even when you're annoyed with them. You'll have to give love to people who don't return it. You'll have to seek joy even in times of stress and struggle.

Whether pursuing Big or Small Meaningful Things, living

your most meaningful life requires effort, time, and facing one's fear. It requires taking leaps of faith and trusting your gut. You will likely never know whether the approach or path you choose is the "right" one, or whether a risk will result in success. But here's the best part about living meaningfully: It doesn't matter. By simply doing something that is meaningful to you, you feel fulfilled.

What Happens When I Start Living in Alignment with My Meaning?

You will experience challenges, roadblocks, fear. When I left my job to take my "mid-career temporary retirement trip," there were collateral consequences: disapproval from others, difficulty maintaining a romantic relationship, financial instability, missing my dog, being far from friends and family on my birthday... the list could go on. Some of those I mindfully accepted before I started. Others presented themselves unexpectedly throughout the experience.

Here's the thing. I could have chosen a different path at any time. I had a sense, however, that despite the ongoing fear, challenges, and roadblocks, in the grand scheme, I was living in alignment with my meaning. I have found that problems feel more manageable, or at least of more value, when they're a result of living life on my terms and in alignment with my soul. Being aware of the "why" of doing something makes roadblocks feel more like growth opportunities and ultimately worthwhile.

You will impact others. By doing your Meaningful Things, I can guarantee that you will affect others. You will almost certainly inspire others to also do soul-aligning things. You will also almost certainly make some people uncomfortable. This resistance, however, is a good sign. It is a sign that your actions are pushing others' outside their comfort zone. The ripple effect of following your bliss will spread farther and wider than you will ever be able to comprehend.

You will feel fulfilled, and that's all you're guaranteed. The business idea you pursued might fail, the friend you forgive may not reciprocate, the rude driver you smiled at might respond with a middle finger, and your trip to Peru may not lead to the self-actualization you were seeking. But regardless of how things ultimately turn out, you will possess the experience and gratification of having lived in alignment with your meaning. In no uncertain terms, that is enough.

You will feel alive. You might feel strong, crazy, fearful, doubtful, different, excited, vibrant. These emotions are the opposite of drab, dull, listless. Whether your Meaningful Things are all the "right" things in the end, you will always possess the experience, the lessons, and the growth. You will live knowing you did everything in your power to *be* alive.

How Do I Figure Out What's Meaningful to Me?

Listen to your gut and seek perspective. The knowledge and wisdom you seek are inside you. Instead of listening to me, or Oprah, or a priest, listen to yourself. Find ways, like being aware of your mortality, to pull your mindset out of the hamster wheel of life and into the bigger, more meaningful picture. Both the Deathbed Meditation and the Delta Assessment in the next chapters will help you tap into your intuition and look at your life objectively and with clarity.

As you complete the two exercises, quiet your mind, take deep breaths, and feel. Let the world and all associated external bullshit quiet down, fade away. Consciously soften the muscles in your chest, soften your heart. Quiet the voices in your head that say this or that isn't possible. Breathe evenly, gathering the breath from deep within your belly and exhale it slowly. Straighten your back and bring your shoulders down. Relax the muscles of your face. Maybe allow the corners of your mouth to turn up ever so slightly into a tiny smile. Allow feelings of well-being to wash over you. Let go of any negativity, especially from your own negative self-talk. Relax.

Open yourself up to what you have to tell yourself. It's your life. Give yourself the chance to live it.

CHAPTER 18:

THE DEATHBED MEDITATION

I created the Deathbed Meditation as a calm, safe, and positive way to access the illuminating life perspective provided by death. I have facilitated this experience for people around the world, in person and online, and found that it brings, above all, clarity and motivation to live authentically.

The meditation is also available in a recorded format on www.youmightdietomorrow.com/deathbed-meditation for your own enjoyment or for sharing with others.

Find a comfortable, quiet space and snuggle in for the experience. Sit or lie down in a position in which you feel at ease and open. You might want to dim the lights, light a candle, enjoy silence, or turn on some soft, instrumental music. If you choose to read the meditation, go slowly and pause for a few moments after each numbered section to close your eyes and visualize. Be kind and gentle with yourself if and when your mind wanders or when you feel challenging emotions. You're about to tap into a beautiful perspective on your life and death.

The Deathbed Meditation

Opening

1. Center yourself. Begin by bringing attention to your breath, your source of life. Gently close your eyes for a few moments.

2. Open your heart, mind, and soul

   - Soften the muscles in your chest. Soften your face. Begin to feel a sense of peace about you as you let go of your tension, worries, and the external world.

3. Relaxation breathing. Be completely in the moment.

   - Take three focused breaths, then begin breathing naturally.

   - As you breathe, feel the beginning, the middle, and the end of each breath. Pause for a moment to recognize the ending of each breath. Everything has an end; everything is fleeting. We must let go. Your breath holds past, present, and future. Each breath comes, and then goes. Each breath has an end but we live in its present.

4. Tell yourself: You are secure. You are strong. You have the answers inside yourself. It's ok to feel worried.

5. Be intimate with this moment now. When it is actually time to die, it will occur in an ordinary living moment, just like this one. Everything, every breath, every moment, every human, will come to an end.

"I am of the nature to grow old; I am of the nature to sicken; I am of the nature to die." —Buddha

Deathbed Scene Creation

1. Begin to let go of your present physical and emotional space, and imagine yourself in a place of immense comfort to you.

- It might be the home of someone in your family, a house on the beach or in the forest, perhaps even in another dimension or a place you've never before been.

2. Pause here with your eyes closed to envision this place in your mind's eye.

- Where are you? What do you see around you? Is it bright and light or cozy and dim? Upon what do you lie, so cozy and safe? Who, if anyone, do you sense to be there with you? Perhaps there is a companion animal present, curled up in bed next to you.

3. Wherever you are, you are profoundly comfortable. Now that you have observed your surroundings, move your

attention to yourself and your consciousness.

4. Take a moment to acknowledge that this is your
deathbed. This is the place you will take your last breaths.
You have been given the gift of spending your last moments
in a comfortable place.

Your Life Review

Knowing you will die soon, take the opportunity to look
back over your life. There is nothing more for you to do but
consider. You begin to look over your life, from the beginning.

1. Think about where you have come from: your family,
your childhood friends, other people from your childhood
who made an impact on you, like aunts, uncles, teachers,
and coaches.

2. Remaining aware of your body and the comfortable, safe
space you are in, think about your experiences, choices, and
what you learned as you became an adult. Salient memories
flicker through your mind's eye.

Eventually, you come to the present moment in your life of
this meditation. This is your moment to reflect on your present
life with the perspective offered by being at the end of it. There
is no expectation, no pride, no fear of embarrassment or failure.
It's just you and your life. Look upon it with the wisdom of death.

1. Think of your relationships. Think of who was most important to you in your life, who you truly loved. The faces of those people may rise up in your mind's eye or grace your mind and heart.

- Looking at those relationships, observe which you tended to and which you allowed to dissipate.

- Consider who you forgave and who you held on to anger toward or kept a grudge against. In death, all extenuating circumstances disappear and only the truth is left in plain sight.

- Objectively, see how you spent your Life Time and energy. Consider how you chose to spend your time here on earth.

  - Think of those you helped.

  - Think of the things you are proud to have created or done.

2. Consider whether you enjoyed your life. Whether you prioritized your own happiness. Whether you openly acknowledged and let your feelings flow, or too often held them back. Whether you took small daily actions to bring joy to your life and to care for your body, mind, and soul.

3. Finally, take a moment to consider what you would have done if you were given the gift of more time.

- What did you tell yourself you couldn't do that you now see you could and should have done? If you could go back, what would you do differently? What's the thing you most regret not having done? Who are the people you could have loved better and more vocally? Which dreams did you put off?

- As you reflect upon your life from the perspective of your deathbed, observe what you feel in your gut. Perhaps it's nostalgia, satisfaction, remorse, gratitude, or regret. Observe these emotions and visceral sensations you might be experiencing. Do not judge them; simply identify.

- If these feelings are uncomfortable, remember you are in a safe space and continue to observe your feelings. Continue to breathe, and sit with whatever is coming up. If you feel yourself judging, try to let go of your judgements. If you feel sad, feel the sadness. If you feel the urge to cry, allow yourself to cry. If you feel anger, feel anger.

Acknowledge the profound perspective you have at this moment and take note of it in your heart, mind, and soul.

Closing and Reflection

Take another breath and allow yourself to come back to the present.

The feelings which arise in this meditation are lessons; they are your teachers and your life instruction manual. In death, everything but truth falls away.

We are here in the present moment, alive, together. You possess power and autonomy in your life. Put your hand over your heart and breathe in. Feel your aliveness with each breath.

You do not have control over when, where, or how you die. What you have control over is how you choose to live until that moment comes. Imagine any fear or worry you have within you transforming into motivation to act; urgency to live while you are alive. What you act on is completely up to you, and you are the only one who can initiate and sustain that action energy before it's too late.

You will die. Live your life so you can die with peace. You are creating your legacy every single moment, and with every decision you make. What matters to you? Listen to that voice.

There is no reason not to follow your heart.

Take a moment to acknowledge your utter insignificance. Let the weight of your constructed self-importance lift from your shoulders. We are gravitationally stuck to a rock spinning through a universe larger than our comprehension. No one really knows what we're doing here. We are stardust. Time happens not just in calendar pages, but in epochs. Everything comes and goes. All things fade. We have only this moment to be alive. We have only one life to create and enjoy. Do not waste this precious resource. Live with urgency.

"Regardless of how much courage it can take to live true to your own path, it will never be as painful as lying on your deathbed with the regret of not having tried." —Bronnie Ware

Be unburdened by the future and the past. We have only now. Smile. You're alive. Now go, *be* alive.

CHAPTER 19

THE DELTA ASSESSMENT

"Make a list of things that make you happy.
Make a list of things you do every day.
Compare the lists.
Adjust accordingly."

-Unknown

Instructions

1. Fold the graph on the next page along the center vertical line so that only the "Importance rating" side is visible (seriously, don't skip this).

2. In the "Importance Rating" column, assign a value of 1-10 for how important each aspect is to your meaningful life, with 10 being extremely meaningful. Do this before proceeding to the next instructions.

3. Now, without looking at the 'importance' values you assigned, flip your folded page and complete the 'Expenditure Rating" column. Assign a value of 1-10 for how much time you expend on each of the aspects listed, with 10 being the greatest amount of time.

4. Finally, score the difference between the two columns. You may have positive or negative numbers and zeroes.

5. Circle the three areas that have the largest score differential. These are the areas in your life which have the greatest delta between what's important to you and how you spend your time and energy.

	Importance rating How important are each of these aspects to your meaningful life? 1=not at all important 10=profoundly important	Expenditure rating How much time and energy do you expend on each of these aspects? 1=no energy at all 10=significant time/energy	
Service & help to others/Giving back			Service & help to others/Giving back
Spouse/partner/ romatic love			Spouse/partner/ romatic love
Family (parents, siblings)			Family (parents, siblings)
Children			Children
Friends			Friends
Being outdoors/being in & exploring nature			Being outdoors/being in & exploring nature
Personal health, e.g. exercise and sleep			Personal health, e.g. exercise and sleep
Creativity/ Self-expression			Creativity/ Self-expression
Enjoyment/Happiness			Enjoyment/Happiness
Work/Career			Work/Career
Financial success			Financial success
Learning/Growth			Learning/Growth
Quiet time/ Meditation/Reflection			Quiet time/ Meditation/Reflection

Reflection: Align Your Actions with Your Meaning

Where are you overspending your time and energy in relation to your values? Where are you underspending?

There are opportunities to do meaningful things every day which we squander in favor of ceding to the daily demands of life — or often, just zoning out. I can promise you that, at the end of my life, I will not value the time I spent mindlessly scrolling through social media posts like a coked-out, bleary-eyed chimpanzee. That's the best case. At worst case, I will look back and profoundly regret the disgusting quantity of hours that I was breathing, my heart beating, life coursing through my veins, that *I chose to zone out on my phone.* The twenty-four hours in a day are fixed. The variable within our control is energy, and how we choose to expend it within that time frame. You can spend the time zoning out on your phone or climbing Mount Everest.

Consider this about energy allocation and prioritization: If I have always dreamed of climbing Mount Everest, but instead spend my time and energy zoning out on my phone, then zoning out is, effectively, my priority. Because the allocation of my energy is within my control, *my expenditure of energy assigns value to whatever I apply it to.*

Let's say you've always wanted to run a marathon, for example, but you never take the time to run, instead filling that time with work, or your kids, or underwater basket weaving. By not spending your finite time currency on training for the marathon, you thereby assign more value to what you did pursue with that time currency.

How you spend your time is the clearest reflection of your priorities.

This isn't necessarily a bad thing. Let's say you've always had a desire to run a marathon, but instead of taking the time to run each day, you spend that time playing with your kids, which you find deeply meaningful. In effect, you are assigning a higher priority or value to being with your children than to training for the marathon.

But if, instead of running, you watch underwater basket weaving reality TV shows which have little meaning for you, there are likely one of three truths about what running (or whichever goal you have) means to you:

1. That thing is not actually important to you.
2. That thing is important to you, but you are prioritizing other things above it.
3. That thing is incredibly important to you, but you are allowing (or using) fear to block yourself from doing it.

Think of something you consider a priority but haven't taken the time to do or start. Which of the above is true?

It is your responsibility to adjust the time energy you expend in each area of your life so that your priorities align with your Meaningful Things.

Sure, there are things we all have to do which might not directly help us in our meaningful pursuits. I call them dentist appointment obligations, things you just have to do — empty the dishwasher, errands, paperwork, work. But it's up to you to vigilantly make sure these things are allotted only the exact quantity of time and energy needed to get them done, and no more. Your time is finite, and if you spend too much time on the dentist appointment obligations, you won't have time for

Meaningful Things.

Which of your obligations are getting far more of your time and attention than they require? Do you really want to run the marathon, or do you think you should run the marathon because you think it will make you appear a certain way to the outside world? If that marathon does feel meaningful to you, then how will you adjust your output of time and energy in order to make it happen?

How would each area of your life change if you knew you were going to die in a year? Is the life you're living worth the price you're paying to live it?

Prioritize, sacrifice what has little meaning to you, be present in your life, and be a ruthless advocate for your values. When you forget, remember that your Life Time is limited — and that life is too short to beat yourself up.

I might die tomorrow.
May I remember this
Every conscious day of my life
May it infuse my actions.
May it inspire me to be my kindest,
Most generous, playful
And loving self.
And when I fail at this,
As I have done today
And do every day:
May it remind me to be kind to myself.

—Lila Donnolo, 2019

CONCLUSION

□

CHAPTER 20:

LIVE TODAY

Living like you might die tomorrow isn't just something you "do," it's a way of being. It is experiencing moments of gratitude for your life so warm and strong you can't help but close your eyes, smile, and lift your face to the sky.

There's a gut feeling that even though you're not always sure you're doing the "right" thing, you are living in a way that makes you feel alive. There is a sense of urgency to do things now and not later. Feet and legs feel stable upon the earth, you are happy to be alive and for the privilege to experience it all.

Death draws out the truth of life and highlights the reality that we're not the center of the universe. You are stuck to a rock which is spinning through space in a universe more extensive than humans yet comprehend. There are 7.5 billion people in the world today. It is estimated that 107 billion people have lived since the beginning of human history. You will live, and then you will die. In the great scheme of things, you are insignificant.

Isn't it great?

It's pretty freeing when you consider the great span of time behind you and in front of you and the tiny blip that you are within that. With that perspective, the reasons we invent for not living our most authentic expression of self seem insignificant and empty. Nothing is permanent. Perfection loses its lead to richness of experience. Now opens to always be the most opportune time.

Everything is constantly in flux, growing, changing, evolving. Ending. We use the phrase "this, too, shall pass" to offer reassurance that a tough time won't last, but it applies to all experience. Both the sad and sweet moments shall pass. That stunning sunset? The sound of your baby's laugh? The dark feeling of grief or depression? The opportunity to help someone? Your very life? This — everything we know, every experience, every moment — too, shall pass.

Impermanence is at the very heart of our existence. This fact will either cause you great suffering or set you free. Will you expect things to stay the same and get frustrated when they do not? If you knew your love would end in heartbreak, would you still open your heart? Would you elect not to be born, knowing you will end as dust?

Impermanence is a source of wild possibility. Thich Nhat Hanh says, "Thanks to impermanence, everything is possible." You can change your life course at any time. Opportunity is endless.

Your life is happening now. And now. And now!

The question begs to be answered, however, if everything could be gone in an instant, why bother? The realization of the impermanence of all beings and things can inspire great zeal or great apathy. This is your choice to actively make.

Apathy is commonly understood to be the state of not caring. One may decide that life is meaningless and to give up the best option. But apathy can also present as a non-choice, the person who lives like that dandelion seed floating in the wind. Hell, in this reactive state, you may even feel overwhelmingly busy with living. Life might feel as if it is so filled up with the busywork and everyday pressures that it's packed to the gills, leaving no time to experience moments that make you feel grateful to be alive. Make no mistake, however. This state of being is a choice. To live one's life in the apathy zone, numb and floating pliantly through life responding to what's loudest or easiest is not usually an active, one-time choice. Rather, it's a passive choice that is made many times per day.

If you are not actively creating your meaningful life, you are living apathetically. You can give up, zone out, or choose to really live before you die. Which do you choose?

Make this choice every single day.

Regardless of how you choose to live, the existential questions persist. No one really knows what we are doing here. Most people who have found their life's purpose are just taking a best guess. In the absence of definite answers, I see little option but to resolve to make enjoying myself my life's purpose. Joy creates joy. Let that be the ripple effect you create in the world.

It is challenging to prioritize seeking happiness, pleasure, joy, and delight. Are you ever about to laugh or cry, and as the emotion comes bubbling up, you consciously (or subconsciously) suppress it? What was almost an uninhibited smile or laugh becomes sheepish or the cry stops at the throat, the sadness or gladness trapped from release. You push it down as if you're doing something bad, like a child caught playing with their mother's makeup. *That wasn't me feeling good, I swear. I promise I'm busy and preoccupied and I haven't taken a moment for myself in ages, we say guiltily, red lipstick smeared on our mouths.*

What a tragedy it is that we stifle the apices of our emotional existence.

Suppress no joy. Don't waste the little time you have suppressing chances to experience pure emotion.

When was the last time you had a spark, an interesting idea or spark for life and actually did something about it? When you didn't pummel it with sandbags of doubts? Or maybe you let the interesting idea see the light of day for a little bit, but later patted it on the head saying, "Let's do this some other time," and shut it in a closet to gather dust. Or your zeal had been tap dancing with a broad smile on stage, but you asked it to step down the moment some guy in the back rolled his eyes and looked back down at his phone.

Steer your life with the abandon and joie de vivre of someone two drinks in. Live with your inhibitions at half-mast, driven by desire and joy rather than worry and fear. Say and do what feels right in the moment. Let unapologetic pleasure be a valid and valiant life purpose. Liberate yourself from self-imposed constraints. Quit complaining and expending energy on figuring out reasons why you can't do what you want to do. Done is better than perfect. You're not in control of the outcome, no matter what you do. So why not try something that lights you up?

No need to keep a flask in your pocket to live like this. Let your mortal perspective help you come alive.

How You Might Live if You Knew You Were Going to Die Soon
(and we could all die soon)

1. You would love openly so the people you love know you love them.
2. You would care less about insignificant things.
3. You would experience the present moment more fully.
4. You would actively enjoy your life.
5. You would feel gratitude for the time you have left to be alive.
6. You would come to terms with your impermanence and fear of death.
7. And finally, you would feel a *sense of urgency* to do all of the above — to live while you're still alive.

Go ahead, start with number 1. Pick up your phone and text or call someone you love to tell them so. No, really — do it now. I'll wait. It's important.

Love. When everything is stripped away — ego, obstinance, anger, fear — we are left with love. It's the base layer of humanity, existing not only between living beings, but everywhere. Love is available to us in every expression of our existence. Love people, animals, experiences, truth, knowledge, growth, challenge, LIFE. To live vibrantly is to live in love with all things, even, no, especially the stuff that feels hard to love. What would it be like to love with abandon?

Love the shit out of life, your family, your friends, that annoying lady on the subway, your dog, your work, the people who have hurt you, and yourself. Forgive and set yourself free. Fall in love with being alive and all the joys and challenges that brings.

Everything has beauty and merit, and you have a profound capacity to love freely and with abandon.

When you love openly, freely, and like you may not get another opportunity to express your love to the people you love, nothing is left on the table. When you live as an expression of love, there will be no regret. Love is our gift and our legacy.

BOB ROSS THE SHIT OUT OF YOUR LIFE. It's your greatest work of art. You are the painter. Your color scheme can start pastel and end up neon. Follow your instincts as you go. Add a purple pet parakeet over here and a golden babbling brook over there.

If you don't start painting now, when will you? Tomorrow? Next year? When you have more money or a more flexible job or when you feel 'ready?' It's easy to think there will always be a tomorrow or a later on. Don't make me repeat the title of this book. Hedge your bet. From the ancient philosopher Seneca: Live immediately.

Give death a big 'fuck you' by living your life with more zeal and joy than you ever have before. Be obstinate about your non-negotiable policy of making your life awesome. Have adventures. Stand on top of the literal or figurative mountains you climb and flip the bird to Death. Play ring-around-the-rosy with your kids (hell, any kids). Let the flush in your cheeks and the sweat on your brow and the smile on your face be a gangster chin nod to your mortality.

Your best bet for cheating death is to really live. To enjoy yourself. To have fun. To help others. To love. And to experience hurt.

Yes, to hurt. To really live, you must take risks. If you aren't occasionally uncomfortable, experience some emotional pain, don't possess some worry that you have made the wrong decision, gone too far, loved too much — you will have regrets when you face death. It's ok; you will make mistakes. But the only antidote to deathbed regret is to live exuberantly and with exaggeration. There are no rewards for living a tepid, timid life. There is no trophy for holding back.

To summarize: How to live like you might die tomorrow

1. Do meaningful shit.
2. Start now.

As a unit of time, life is unfixed. Unknown. Unreliable. We can measure and know the duration and endpoint of a minute, but the duration of life is only measurable in retrospect. I know the point from which I was born and began, but I know not my endpoint.

How does one operate under such ambiguous conditions? There's only one productive way: Operate as if the deadline is tomorrow. Today, even. If you don't know when the boss is going to ask for the work, you've got to have it ready immediately. There is no room for procrastination. The deadline is the sure thing here. The variable is how you operate until that expiration date arrives.

Jane Goodall said, "In my life right now, I'm eighty. There is so much left to do. So I would like to go back and give myself a bit longer, but as it is, I don't know how long I have to live, but certainly it is that every year takes me closer to the end, whenever that end is. And so there is this feeling of desperation - there's so many places I want to go, so many people I want to talk to, and so many hearts I want to reach."

Ms. Goodall feels desperate to live now, at 80, but she could have been given her deadline at 20 or 40 or 79. Don't wait until you are "old" to feel desperate to live life. Live today. Live now.

Life is made up of moments, minutes, hours, days. How you choose to spend these units of time is how you choose to spend your life. There's a video by Ze Frank, "The Time You Have (in JellyBeans)." It depicts, in a rainbow of more than 28,835 colorful jelly-beans, the number of days in the American life expectancy. Then, a hand removes groups of jelly-beans to represent the days spent taking care of work, sleep, going to the bathroom, and all the other necessary responsibilities of being alive. What's left is a small pile of jelly-beans. The hand then halves that pile and halves it again, representing the chance we all have of a shorter-than-average life expectancy. The rainbow sweet pile of life, love, sunny days, puppy cuddles, and breath in your lungs dwindles even further until one jelly-bean remains. He closes with this:

"What if you just had one more day? What are you going to do today?"

"While we are postponing, life speeds by." —Seneca

Death and the awareness that it can come at any time is your kick in the pants out of decision paralysis. What death offers is twofold: Urgency to act and clarity about what those acts should be.

Death is the non-negotiable end of the road with a glaring street light that shines away the trifles of life. We all have to answer to it with our soul bared.

We must remember that there isn't just one path or one perfect route. We possess the prerogative to change our minds at any time. A ship sets its navigation point and begins sailing toward that point. But as it goes along, appearing to be traveling in a straight line, it's actually making thousands of mini cross-corrections in response to wind, waves, and obstructions. But still, it follows the trajectory of where it's meant to go on the voyage. If a big storm comes or the captain changes their mind? Simple. Change the navigation point, adjust the instruments, and press on.

Set your course toward living a meaningful life and start down the path. Cross-correct as you go, iterate, change paths entirely, but never give up the dogged pursuit of living authentically before you die.

JOIN THE MOVEMENT

Visit www.youmightdietomorrow.com and follow Kate and the movement on social media for more inspiring content:

- Daily inspiration to help you live more alive
- YOU MIGHT DIE TOMORROW, SO LIVE TODAY merchandise (t-shirts, stickers, tote bags, mugs, and more)
- More books (coming soon)

@youmightdietomorrow on Instagram
@You Might Die Tomorrow on Facebook

Kate delivers keynote speeches and workshops globally.

NOTES ON SOURCES

Chapter Zero: Exposure Therapy

7   Kid killed by golf club: "Youth Killed as Club's Shaft Pierces Heart." *The New York Times,* July 11, 1994.

7   Brazilian farmer killed by cow: Quinn, Rob. "Cow Crashes through Roof, Kills Sleeping Man." *USA Today,* July 5, 2015. https://www.usatoday.com/story/news/world/2013/07/15/newser-cow-kills-man/2517321/.

7   Girl killed by elephant: Etehad, Melissa. "7-Year-Old Girl Dies after Elephant Throws Stone in Morocco Zoo." *The Washington Post,* July 28, 2016. https://www.washingtonpost.com/news/worldviews/wp/2016/07/28/seven-year-old-girl-dies-after-elephant-throws-stone-in-morocco-zoo/.

9   "Most people are not ready for death..." quote: Bukowski, Charles. *The Captain Is Out to Lunch and the Sailors Have Taken Over the Ship.* Ecco, 2002.

11   The universal fear of death: Bryant, Clifton D. *Handbook of Death and Dying*. SAGE Publications, Inc, 2003.

14   Tyler Durden: Palahniuk, Chuck. *Fight Club: a Novel*. W.W. Norton & Company, 2018.

Chapter 7: Introduction to Part II

86   Post-traumatic growth: Tedeschi, R. G. Calhoun, L. G.. "Trauma & transformation: Growing in the aftermath of suffering." Thousand Oaks, CA: *SAGE Publications, Inc.*, 1995. doi: 10.4135/9781483326931

86   Post-traumatic growth: Tedeshi, R.G., & Calhoun, L.G.. "Posttraumatic Growth: Conceptual Foundation and Empirical Evidence." *Philadelphia, PA: Lawrence Erlbaum Associates*, 2004.

86   "No mud, no lotus" quote: Hanh, Thich Nhat. *No Mud, No Lotus*. Parallax Press, 2014.

Chapter 9: The Survivor's Perspective

95   4-15%; Prevalence of NDEs: *Key NDE Facts*. International Association of Near-Death Experiences, 27 Aug. 2017, https://iands.org/ndes/about-ndes/key-nde-facts21.html?start=1.

95-   Anita Moorjani NDE account: Moorjani, Anita.
96   *Dying to Be Me*. Hay House, Inc., 2012.

97 "They're profoundly appreciative of being alive…" quote by Dr. Kenneth Ring; 1 in 3 people have tran scendental NDE: Bass, Sharon L. "CONNECTICUT Q & A: KENNETH RING; 'You Never Recover Your Original Self'." The New York Times, Aug. 1988.

97 Orne, R. M. (1995), "The meaning of survival: The early aftermath of a near-death experience." *Res. Nurs. Health*, 18: 239-247. doi:10.1002/nur.4770180307

Chapter 10: What Not to Do

99 2009 publishing of Ware's article: Ware, Bronnie. *The Top Five Regrets of the Dying.* 2009, https://bronnieware. com/regrets-of-the-dying/.

100 Heidegger's two modes of being: Korab-Karpowicz, W.J. "Martin Heidegger (1889—1976)." *Internet Encyclopedia of Philosophy*, https://www.iep.utm.edu/ heidegge/.

101 "And every day, the world will drag you by the hand," quote: Thomas, Iain. *I Wrote This for You.* Central Avenue Publishing, 2017.

106 "One day, you will learn how to give…" quote: DeMulder, Sierra. *Tumblr*, https://sierrade mulder.tumblr.com/poetry.

107   "Smoke Alarm" lyrics: Blanton, Carsie. "Smoke Alarm."
Idiot Heart. 2012.

110   "Deep within, they longed to laugh…" quote: Ware,
Bronnie. The Top Five Regrets of the Dying: A Life
Transformed by the Dearly Departing. Hay House, Inc.,
2012.

112   "Live life not in the pursuit of happiness…" quote:
Sadhguru. *Life and Death in One Breath.* Jaico Publishing
House.

112   "How can you live now without…" quote: Yalom, Irvin
D. *Staring at the Sun.* W F Howes, 2010.

Chapter 13: Our Denial of Death

123   "Adults who are racked with…" quote: Yalom, Irvin D.
Staring at the Sun. W F Howes, 2010.

124   *Gone With the Wind*: Mitchell, Margaret. *Gone With the
Wind.* Macmillan Publishers, 1936.

124   Life expectancy 34 years old in 1800s England:
Galor, Oded; Moav, Omer. "Natural Selection and
the Evolution of Life Expectancy" (PDF). *Brown
University Working Paper.* 2005.

124 Infant mortality rates: *Achievements in Public Health, 1900-1999: Healthier Mothers and Babies.* Centers for Disease Control, 1999, https://www.cdc.gov/mmwr/preview/mmwrhtml/mm4838a2.htm.

125 Dr. Thomas Holmes and embalming history: Tom Hickman, *Death - A User's Guide*, London 2002, p. 102.

126 Benedictine monks' caskets: Barnes, Robert. "Louisiana's Casket-Making Monks Declare Victory with Appeals Court Ruling." *The Washington Post*, Oct. 2012.

128 Gilgamesh: Sanders, N.K. (translation). *The Epic of Gilgamesh.* Penguin Classics, 1960.

129 Chinese emperor's poisoning death: Wright, David Curtis. *The History of China*, Greenwood Publishing Group, 2001.

130 Young blood transfusions: Robbins, Rebecca. "Young-Blood Transfusions Are on the Menu at Society Gala". *Scientific American*, 2018.

130 One-third of patients over 60: Wiseman, Heather. *One Third of Elderly Patients Receive Futile Treatment before They Die.* Palliative Care Australia, 2016. https://palliativecare.org.au/one-third-of-elderly-patients-receive-futile-treatment-before-they-die.

130 Medicalization of end-of-life: M Cardona-Morrell, JCH Kim, RM Turner, M Anstey, IA Mitchell, K Hillman, "Non-beneficial treatments in hospital at the end of life: a systematic review on extent of the problem," *International Journal for Quality in Health Care*, Volume 28, Issue 4, September 2016, Pages 456–469, https://doi.org/10.1093/intqhc/mzw060.

130 One-third of American adults: Andrews, Michelle. *Many Avoid End-Of-Life Care Planning, Study Finds.* NPR, 2017, https://www.npr.org/sections/health-shots/2017/08/02/540669492/many-avoid-end-of-life-care-planning-study-finds.

130 No official directive for ending CPR: Torke, Alexia M., Bledsoe, Patricia, Wocial, Lucia D., Bosslet, Gabriel T., Helft, Paul R. "CEASE: A Guide for Clinicians on How to Stop Resuscitation Efforts." *American Thoracic Society Annals*, vol. 12, no. 3, 1 Mar. 2015.

131 80% of Americans; most Americans prefer: *Where Do Americans Die?* Stanford School of Medicine, https://palliative.stanford.edu/home-hospice-home-care-of-the-dying-patient/where-do-americans-die/.

Chapter 14: Understand the Fear to Overcome It

133 Thich Nhat Hanh, fear: Hanh, Thich Nhat. *No Mud, No Lotus.* Parallax Press, 2014.

133   Blake Mycoskie, fear: Mycoskie, Blake. *Start Something that Matters.* Spiegel & Grau, 2012.

134-   Ernest Becker's theory: Becker, Ernest. *The Denial of*
136   *Death.* The Free Press, 1973.

135,   Terror Management Theory (TMT): Solomon, Sheldon,
142   Greenberg, Jeff, Pyszczynski, Tom. *The Worm at the Core: On the Role of Death in Life.* Penguin RandomHouse, 2015.

137-   Symbolic immortality: Lifton, Robert Jay, Olson, Eric.
141   *Living and Dying.* Wildwood House, 1974.

137-   Symbolic immortality: Lifton, Robert. *The Broken*
141   *Connection: On Death and the Continuity of Life.* Simon and Schuster, 1979.

143-   Basketball study: Zestcott, Colin & Lifshin, Uri &
144   Helm, Peter & Greenberg, Jeff. "He Dies, He Scores: Evidence That Reminders of Death Motivate Improved Performance in Basketball." *Journal of Sport and Exercise Psychology.* 2016. 38. 1-40. 10.1123/jsep.2016-0025.

144   Self-esteem and TMT: Burke, Brian L., et al. "Two Decades of Terror Management Theory: A Meta-Analysis of Mortality Salience Research." *Personality and Social Psychology Review*, vol. 14, no. 2, May 2010, doi:10.1177/1088868309352321.

144- September 11 responses research: Grant, Adam
145   & Wade-Benzoni, Kimberly. "The hot and cool
      of death awareness at work: Mortality cues,
      aging, and self-protective and prosocial motivations."
      Academy of Management Review, 2009. 34. 600-622.
      10.5465/AMR.2009.44882929.

Chapter 15: How to Hack Your Fear of Death to Live Your Most Meaningful Life

147- Fear and road trip metaphor: Gilbert, Elizabeth.
148   *Big Magic: Creative Living Beyond Fear.*
      Bloomsbury Publishing, 2015.

148   Fred Rogers quote: Farmer-Kris, Deborah. *The Timeless Teachings of Mister Rogers*. PBS, 2017, https://www.pbs. org/parents/thrive/the-timeless-teachings-of-mister- rogers.

149   Prosocial effects of mortality awareness: Gailliot, Matthew & Stillman, Tyler & Schmeichel, Brandon & Maner, Jon & Plant, Ashby. "Mortality Salience Increases Adherence to Salient Norms and Values." *Personality & social psychology bulletin*, 2008. 34. 993- 1003. 10.1177/0146167208316791.

149   Prosocial effects of mortality awareness: Vail, Kenneth & Juhl, Jacob & Arndt, Jamie & Vess, Matthew & Routledge, Clay & Rutjens, Bastiaan. "When Death is Good for Life: Considering the Positive

Trajectories of Terror Management." *Personality and social psychology review : an official journal of the Society for Personality and Social Psychology, Inc.* 2012. 16. 303-29. 10.1177/1088868312440046.

149-   Prosocial effects of mortality awareness: Vail, Kenneth
150   & Juhl, Jacob. "An Appreciative View of the Brighter Side of Terror Management Processes." *Social Sciences.* 2015. 4. 1020-1045. 10.3390/socsci4041020.

150   Leaving a legacy neutralizes death fears: Sligte, Daniel J., et al. "Leaving a Legacy Neutralizes Negative Effects of Death Anxiety on Creativity." *Personality and Social Psychology Bulletin*, vol. 39, no. 9, Sept. 2013, doi:10.1177/0146167213490804.

151   How to handle a bear attack: "Bear Encounters in the Backcountry." Bear Smart Society. Accessed January 5, 2019. http://www.bearsmart.com/play/bear-encounters/.

Chapter 16: Invite Death Awareness into Your Life

157   "Reflecting on death needn't be frightening or morbid..." quote: Rinpoche, Sogyal. *The Tibetan Book of Living and Dying: The Spiritual Classic & International Bestseller: Revised and Updated Edition.* HarperOne, 2002.

157   Death in Buddhism: Jagaro, Ajahn. *True Freedom.* Buddhadhamma Foundation, 1996.

158   Ecclesiastes passage: *The Holy Bible.* New International Version. Grand Rapids: Zondervan. House, 1984.

158   Ossuary in Rome: Korn, Frank J. *Hidden Rome.* Vol. 1. Paulist Press, 2002.

158-   Bhutanese happiness: Brooks, Arthur C. "To Be Happier,
159   Start Thinking More About Your Death." *The New York Times*, 2016.

160   Cremation statistics: *Statistics.* National Funeral Directors' Association, 2019, https://www.nfda.org/news/statistics.

160   UK #1 funeral song choice: Silverman, Rosa. "Baby Boomers Jazz Up Their Funerals With Monty Python and Fancy Dress." *The Telegraph*, 2014. https://www.telegraph.co.uk/news/picturegalleries/howaboutthat/11243943/Baby-boomers-jazz-up-their-funerals-with-Monty-Python-and-fancy-dress.html.

160-   Norma Bauerschmidt story: Bauerschmidt, Tim and
161   Little, Ramie. *Driving Miss Norma.* HarperOne, 2017.

Chapter 17: Live in Alignment With Your Meaning

166   Meaning and logotherapy: Frankl, Viktor. *Man's Search for Meaning.* Beacon Press, 1959.

Other sources

Sherman, Edmund. *Contemplative Aging: A Way of Being in Later Life.* Gordian Knot, 2010.

Fowler, James & Christakis, Nicholas. "Dynamic Spread of Happiness in a Large Social Network: Longitudinal Analysis Over 20 Years in the Framingham Heart Study." *BMJ (Clinical research ed.)*, 2008. .337. a2338. 10.1136/bmj.a2338.

Levasseur, Oona, et al. "The Multidimensional Mortality Awareness Measure and Model: Development and Validation of a New Self-Report Questionnaire and Psychological Framework." *OMEGA - Journal of Death and Dying*, vol. 70, no. 3, Feb. 2015, pp. 317–341, doi:10.1177/0030222815569440.

Steinman, Christopher T., and John A. Updegraff. "Delay and Death-Thought Accessibility: A Meta-Analysis." *Personality and Social Psychology Bulletin*, vol. 41, no. 12, Dec. 2015, doi:10.1177/0146167215607843.

Studerus E, Gamma A, Vollenweider FX. "Psychometric Evaluation of the Altered States of Consciousness Rating Scale (OAV)." *PLoS ONE, 2010.* 5(8): e12412. https://doi.org/10.1371/journal.pone.0012412.

ACKNOWLEDGEMENTS

I'm alive, so the first people I have to thank are my parents, Brian and Susan. Thank you for making that happen and for supporting my life choices, many of which no doubt give you pause. Thank you to my siblings, Kelly and Tom, for alternating love, friendship, and giving me a run for my money.

To Dan Fredinburg and his family. Thank you for showing me that living authentically is the only way to truly live and the best way to positively impact the world. The ripples of inspiration created by Dan's life still have me — and so many people around the world — completely drenched. They continue to wave on.

To Melissa and Scott Saville, thank you for breaking from the blueprint to live life on the High Line. I treasure your support and you're always my salty source of inspiration.

To the families of Stephen Carney, Mallory Rae Dies, and Ivan Bilenky, thank you. Stephen was an example of how to be unapologetically oneself. Mallory and Ivan taught me that having fun is a completely valid and valiant life's purpose.

Para a minha mãe Brasileira, Sueli. Obrigado por criando seu filho quem é tão especial, e, do fundo do meu coração, eu que agradeço por ser meu anjo do suporte e amor.

To Jessica Cooper: thanks to you, I had a person with a big heart, those all-important Psy. D. letters, and wise perspective on my book. Your husband, Daniel, isn't so bad either.

Hey, Ron Seybold, look! I finally finished the book! Thank you for patiently coaching me to get to that all-important earnest and green first draft.

To my editor, Emma Borges-Scott, thank you for bringing me down to Earth and making my odd blend of bluntness and idealistic optimism palatable. You are a kind, gifted editor.

Y'all, writing a book — and living life according to one's bliss and meaning — is damn fulfilling but damn hard. Thank you to the people who have opened their home to me, my dog, and the various iterations of this book: Mom and Dad, Tara, Caitlin, and to everyone who has shared love and support with me and my nontraditional life choices along the way.

Finally, thank you to everyone who has shared their story of living vibrantly with an arm around mortality, everyone who has faithfully read the blog, and the many people who have bought stickers and shirts to rock for inspiration. Keep spreading the magic. Thank you.

At 30 years old, Kate Manser realized an important truth: Remembering that you might die tomorrow is the best inspiration to live today. After experiencing this radical shift in perspective, Kate quit her job at Google to build YOU MIGHT DIE TOMORROW, her movement to inspire people at every age to really live before they die. The movement has grown to a fanbase including an anonymous individual who spray-painted the logo on a building in Argentina, the person who hired Kate to speak to the employees of Facebook, and the thousands of people around the world who have the sticker on their cars, laptops, and bathroom mirrors.

Find more of her work at www.youmightdietomorrow.com. This is Kate's debut book and, as long as she's still kicking, she has many more to come.

Made in United States
North Haven, CT
15 March 2023

34083080R00139